THE

THE BLOODBUS

TALES FROM THE GLASGOW BUSES

BY
THE DRIVER

BLACK & WHITE PUBLISHING

First published 2007
by Black & White Publishing Ltd
29 Ocean Drive, Edinburgh EH6 6JL

ISBN 978 1 84502 176 4

3 5 7 9 10 8 6 4 2   08 09 10

Text copyright © The Driver 2007

The right of The Driver to be identified as
author of this work has been asserted by him
in accordance with the Copyright, Designs
and Patents Act 1988.

British Library Cataloguing in Publication Data:
A catalogue record for this book is available
from the British Library.

Typeset by Ellipsis Books Ltd., Glasgow
Printed and bound by Creative Print and Design Ltd

CONTENTS

'We'd better get back, 'cause it'll be dark soon, and they mostly come at night . . . mostly.'

Rebecca 'Newt' Jorden, *Aliens* (1986)

1
THE BIG BANG

Wearing my crisp new uniform and shiny shoes, I arrived early at the depot today for my first shift as a bus driver. Stepping warily through the gates I immediately noticed that the air was thick with diesel fumes and gratuitous swearing. Billowing, nebulous, mucky clouds of blue smoke and even bluer prose swirled around the bus yard; everything was hazy, everything was 'fucked!'

It wasn't just drivers, though. There were other, more unearthly shapes, moving and profaning wildly through those wispy tendrils. As I got closer, I observed them to be grubby little men in orange boiler suits, walking to and fro, carrying filthy tools and even filthier bits of bus. It looked like the contract for bus maintenance had gone to Willy Wonka and his gang of Oompa Loompas.

Now in the depot office, I fought my way to the desk through a crush of other drivers to be assigned a bus. Despite all the bustle and shouting, it was a quiet voice that claimed my attention.

'Are you new?' asked the voice, a little too close to my ear than was necessary. I turned to face the bearded and bespectacled speaker. He seemed fairly benign, grandfatherly almost, but his piercing stare suggested some concealed motivation.

'Yes, I've just started this morning.'

'Pleased to meet you. I'm Driver Kisses (name changed),

the garage pervert.' He reached out his hand and I made the mistake of shaking it. 'I'm your worst nightmare! I'm the man your parents warned you about! I'm the Devil!' and with that, he puckered up, pulled me forward and planted a great slobbering kiss on my right cheek. The feeling of warm beard rasping against my face was quite unsettling and not easily forgotten, like a damp kitchen scourer with lips. How very continental.

'Welcome to the depot. But just watch yourself out there, 'coz I will be!' said Driver Kisses. I looked around to other drivers for help but they just carried on as though nothing had happened.

What had I let myself in for here? I had committed no crime yet already I felt like the prison play bitch. Prank or not, that had better not happen again. Hot fur pounding against my face will always leave a bad taste in my mouth.

'Kisses claims another victim!' exclaimed a bystander, eventually. 'Don't worry mate, he gets everyone!' said another driver. 'He got me too when I started!' said someone else. Common to all these drivers was a forlorn sense of resignation, like heffers bemoaning the branding iron. Standing there, a victim amongst victims, I had taken one soggy step towards becoming part of the herd. My initiation had begun.

Eventually I was assigned a bus and a route. I thought I was doing the run that went to Paisley, an easy route to navigate on my first day, made easier by the fact that I had gone out in my car the day before and tied yellow ribbons around every lamp post. But no, the first piece of work on that particular duty went to somewhere I'd never even heard of.

'Lindsayfield? Wait a minute, I don't know how to get to Lindsayfield! I've not been route-trained on this run!' I said to Jelly Baby behind the desk.

'That's a bastard, innit?' he replied, without a shade of sympathy.

'I mean, what if I take a wrong turn and hit a low bridge or something?'

'Life's a bitch,' he said, nodding his knuckled forehead. 'Lindsayfield is in East Kilbride. Look, here's a list of all the streets on the route. Now go drive,' said Jelly Baby.

'But . . . shit!' I whimpered.

'Oh, you're not gonna make him do it, are you?' argued Driver Kisses on my behalf. 'He's just started today!'

'My hands are tied!' said Jelly Baby. 'I've got no other drivers to cover it. He'll just have to do it.'

Driver Chucklemumble, who overheard the conversation, offered some golden advice from all his years of experience: 'Juth athk your punterth for directionth if yer not thoor where tae go, theh! theh!'

'What? Ask the punters?' I asked, incredulous.

'Aye, they're yooth tae it, theh! theh! Happenth all the thime,' said Chucklemumble.

I thanked him for his advice but inwardly I was feeling more apprehensive than ever. I hoped my jitters didn't show as I walked out into the yard to locate my bus. As I searched, I noticed that the body panels of many buses were peppered with dozens of scars and dimples. Collision damage maybe? They worried me.

Eventually I found my assigned bus, a big old Volvo double decker, and fired it up. The brute stank of piss and mould and was gradually filling up with the exhaust fumes from the bus parked next to it. Although I'd never been one for horticulture, I was quite taken by the vigour with which a bloom of moss was colonising the rubber window seals. People actually pay to travel on these things? There were some safety checks I *should* have completed and coolant I *should* have put into the radiator, but my state of high-fluster and the choking fumes hastened my departure from the depot somewhat.

So, there I was, let loose on the road in a double decker bus for the first time. I had only just scraped a pass in my PSV test a couple of weeks before and was not at all confident behind the wheel. As I drove along with my nose in a map, trying to find the terminus where I was due to start 'In Service', I clipped a car wing mirror, struck numerous kerbs and knocked a traffic cone into the other side of the road. A bull in a china shop would have looked like a dainty ballerina compared to my antics.

After several wrong turns, I got to the Knightswood terminus twenty minutes later than advertised and noticed a large group of sour faces had built up. The most sour of them was a little blue-rinsed pensioner who immediately hit me with, 'Call this a bus service? Do you know how long I've been standing here? Are you lot oan strike or something? This is scandalous! Scandalous!'

I thought back to my training. How did the company instruct us in how best to deal with difficult passengers? Oh, yeah, they didn't. All I remembered from Bus Driver Training School was a little skinny guy in a blue shirt standing in front of a room of new recruits blabbering on about the ticket machine before finishing with, 'By the way, Glasgow bus drivers call problem pensioners "muppets", because they come in all shapes and sizes.'

Think I just had my first 'muppet'.

What's worse was, when all the snapping had finished and the passengers finally settled themselves into their seats, I had to open my cab door, sheepishly turn round to them and say, 'Um, I don't know where I'm going, could someone possibly direct me?'

'Aw! Christ! I'm goannie be late for ma work!' yelled a high-vizzed worky man in clumpy boots. This wasn't the start to my bus driving career that I'd hoped for. I wanted to provide a valuable service to the community. I wanted to be the bus driver who was always there on time with a smile on his face. The driver who could always be counted on to get people to their destination safely and on time. I wanted to be Wonder Driver. Yet here I was, way behind schedule, without a clue where to go, and definitely not smiling. Wonder Driver? *Witless* Driver more like.

Then, an unexpected change of luck. A heavily pregnant woman came waddling down the bus and agreed to stand beside me and give directions. Yes! Santa Clause may have been relieved to have Rudolph's shiny red nose guide him through the fog but his relief was nothing compared to my elation at having a sticky out belly button point the way through Knightswood.

It worked very well too. *Turn left here, turn right there. Dodge the wheelie bin.* The nasty, tight, twisted streets of Knightswood would have been very intimidating without my abdominous co-pilot. Even when I accidentally slammed into kerbs and the high-vizzed worky guy shouted, 'Christ!' my rotund helper mildly carried on her instructions as though the sudden jolts were merely babies hiccups. Until, that is, we came upon the bin lorry.

He was further up the street and heading my way. Because of the parked cars and wheelie bins on the pavement, there was simply no way we could pass each other. So I stopped and he stopped. I looked at him and he looked at me. Then I inched forward a bit, and he did likewise. Something had to give. Someone was going to have to reverse, but who was going to blink first? It was like two cowboys squaring up at high noon. With deserted streets, it was as though the townsfolk of Tombstone were at home, peeking out through shuttered windows to see who would walk away from this duel. It was like Whoo-ee-oo-ee-oo, whah, whah, whah . . . Even my knocked-up guide decided to sit this one out and waddled away up the bus for a seat.

Now, I don't know if bin lorries have timetables, but buses most certainly do and I was now almost thirty minutes behind schedule. So after a few minutes of staring each other out, I blinked. I caved in. But I did not reverse. Instead, I mounted the kerb and tried to squeeze past, even though I wasn't entirely sure my bus was going to fit. My suspicions were realised when I accidentally clipped a wheelie bin, knocking it over with a loud bang. Oops! With the wheelie bin out the way, I just had room to squeeze past, but I noticed that the black bin bag that had plopped out of the

Sorry, mate!

wheelie bin ruptured after hitting the ground: soggy cornflakes boxes, empty tin cans and reams of brown-stained kitchen roll spewed out and billowed down the street.

The look on the bin men's faces was a picture as they flapped around with their arms in the air like quarrelling apes. One even gave me the middle finger. Yes, they knew what I knew: if they did not clean up the mess then local residents would most likely complain about those terrible bin men leaving mounds of garbage in the street on collection day.

I did feel genuinely bad about that. Even after the pregnant woman came back down the bus and continued to direct me into the city centre, I couldn't help but wonder if I should have perhaps stopped and helped them clean it up.

'Whit? No! No! No!' shouted Driver Chucklemumble when I told him what happened in the greasy depot canteen later on. 'Juth you worry aboot gettin' yer buth through! Dae whit ye have tae dae and don't let yer punterth get tae ye! Ethpethilly don't be gettin' oot yer cab tae clean up crap oot o' wheelie binth. That'th no your joab! Theh! theh!' There was a rumble of assent from other drivers around the table. 'It'th every man for himthelf oot there!'

Every man for himself? Wasn't that why the world was in the state it's in? But, damn it, it worked. It got results.

Well, today was definitely an eye opener. On arriving home, I made straight for the fridge and pulled the cap from a bottle of Grolsch. I just sat and stared into space for a while and reflected on the day's events. If there's one thing I learned after my first shift, it was that bus driving was going to be a hell of a lot of fun. Whether I liked it or not.

Oh, and to bring sandwiches tomorrow. That slop shop of indigestible misery that passed for a canteen should be avoided at all costs.

2
THE LITTLE DOINK

Well, it's been a long and nerve grinding week but I'm still going. Despite Jelly Baby's best efforts of springing routes on me that I don't know, I've just got used to asking passengers for directions and developed a thick skin to their huffy comments. I've had more East Kilbride runs again this week, but this particular one finished somewhere called 'Greenhills'. I was hoping I could get the bus through all those roundabouts in one piece.

There have already been a few times when I felt like simply jumping out the bus and going home. These feelings were augmented by the demise of other new drivers who joined the company at the same time as myself. One was an ex-squaddie who took off his tie and threw it at Jelly Baby when he was given a route he didn't know. 'I've already been sick twice today with nerves,' he said. 'Punters snap at you for bugger all! You even get honked by cars just for putting your indicator on! I'm not cut out for this job!' And with that, he turned round and left. A tour of Iraq, no problem. A tour of East Kilbride, no chance!

Now driving one of the depot's older vehicles, I navigated my way through the notorious Drumchapel area of Glasgow. It was actually a relief to leave that terminus because the unearthly shouts and screams in the distance made my skin crawl. I also wished the bus was equipped with CCTV cameras because I didn't like the look of those loitering youths or 'neds' as they are known. Other drivers had advised me never to ask neds for directions under any circumstances or I'd probably end up in Inverness. Then they regaled me with horror stories of bus vandalism and abusive behaviour from neds up 'the Drum', so I was relieved that my first run through the area was reasonably uneventful.

Having reached the city centre, I concluded that it's the width of the bus that causes most manoeuvring headaches, not the length. The vehicle takes up the whole girth of the road, so when someone walks down Renfield Street and tries to squeeze past one of those litter bins that are positioned right at the edge of the pavement, there are often screams of panic when a bus whistles past and makes off with the hairs on their arse.

With me still being a new driver, I found myself quite unable to get to grips with road positioning. Having struck kerbs, bus stop poles and a wheelie bin, every journey was a turbulent roller-coaster ride that had my passengers gripping their seats in unabashed terror. But, this being Friday night, with drunken louts falling about in the middle of the road with rubbery abandon, I sensed that I would have more than arse hair on my windscreen before the end of the shift.

Unsurprisingly, I was running late and felt inclined to apologize profusely to all my passengers. I had spent too much time hunting for empty beer cans under the seats and squashing them flat so they didn't roll around when I turned corners. It's strange to think that in spite of all the snapping from disgruntled passengers, it was simply people dropping detritus on the bus floor that was really starting to annoy me about dealing with the public. Mind you, I did find an empty bottle of Buckfast that had been fastened securely to the floor by a large glob of chewing gum. Clearly, all those sulphites in Buckfast hadn't destroyed all of his brain cells yet.

Like a runaway wrecking ball, I tumbled down Renfield Street paying only cursory attention to traffic lights. The brakes were really jolty and grabby so I thought it was probably best not to use them. Besides, whenever I did stop, a passing group of rowdy drunks would indulge in some naughtiness by pressing the outside emergency door open button or run round the back of the bus and open the emergency door. It brought back terrible memories of being a kid when the school bully used to sneak up behind me in the gym hall and pull down my shorts in front of all the girls. It seems that, at the weekend, any red traffic light is your mortal foe.

The lights up ahead had just turned from green to amber, but I had already decided there was no way I was going to stop and allow myself to be de-briefed again by those passing oafs. They had got me out the cab twice already to close the rear emergency door and I was damned if I was going to allow them their hat-trick. So I stabbed at the accelerator and shot across the junction at red, taking only a single honk from the line of traffic that was forced to brake. Oops! Well, at least I got away from the unruly drunks. But only to run into more! Literally!

I was so fraught about getting out of harm's way that I hadn't noticed the posse of girlie revellers on the other side of the junction. They had clearly left their high-heeled poise in the last bar they had visited and were now doing the drunken zombie-shuffle toward the next. The pavement was very crowded and the wobbliest girlie wearing the silly big rabbit ears on her head kept stepping out on to the road to pass people. With me now doing almost 30mph towards her (which is light speed for a bus on Renfield Street), I braked and honked and braked some more, but I realised with growing horror that my brakes just weren't going to stop me in time. Hopefully, with those big furry ears, she would hear my horn and get herself back on to the pavement before I squished her right into the ground.

Unfortunately, my bus horn was quieter than a kitten's meow and, despite the severity of the situation, it almost made me laugh. It was only the loud squealing of my brakes that finally made her look round. Oh, the scream she produced could have split rock! All her friends joined in too, like a warning call spreading through a flock of spooked tits.

Miss Rabbit Ears panicked and scrambled for the sanctuary of the pavement. But she was naturally unsteady on her feet and one of those big green litter bins was in the way, impeding her even more. She pulled herself up against the bin and stood on tiptoes as the front end of my bus thundered down on her.

Doink!

Despite missing the majority of her fleshy wobbliness, I just clipped the back of her elbow, sending her arm flailing out in front of her. I watched in my wing mirror as she rubbed furiously at it. Strangely, it was only her friends who screamed this time.

The official procedure now was to stop the bus and check on the injured pedestrian. It was possible that a paramedic may have to be called to give her the once-over and, depending on her condition, the police may get involved and pursue a charge of careless driving against me. Then there would be the inevitable disciplinary hearing with the depot gaffer.

Wait a minute. Paramedic? Police? Disciplinary hearing? I

definitely didn't like the sound of all that! There are not many jobs that can land you in serious doo-doo like this just because of a single moment's thoughtlessness. Besides, I was just new with the company and didn't want to be making a bad name for myself so soon. So, heaven help me, I legged it! I just shot through the junction. And the next. And the next.

Initially, I figured the rabbit girl might have picked up a little bruise as a result of my vehicular inexperience. But as time passed, and my conscience gnawed at me, her injury grew in severity from a little bruise to a dislocated elbow. As I passed through Rutherglen I convinced myself that I had broken one of her bones, and by the time I finally reached the Greenhills terminus, I had severed her entire arm just below the shoulder.

*I'd gladly donate one of my arms to her just to salve my own conscience,
as long as she doesn't mind hairy knuckles.*

When I arrived back at the depot, guilt was really getting the better of me. I thought it better to fess up now in case Miss Rabbit Ears had already phoned through a complaint.

So, I explained to Jelly Baby behind the desk what happened and he stuck a form under my nose to fill in. After settling myself in the depot canteen with a coffee from the vending machine, I tried to figure out how to recount the incident without placing the blame entirely with myself. What it boiled down to was this: crap buses on tight timetables don't mix very well with drunk pedestrians on crowded streets. But I had a feeling the boss wouldn't like that.

'What 'ave ye done?' asked a toothless Driver Gollum as he came into the canteen for his break. A bit of a live wire was Gollum who immediately grabbed my report away from me and read over it, shaking his big balding head.

'I accidentally doinked someone on Renfield Street tonight,' I said.

'Hmmm. You're new, mate, ain't you?'

'Yup.'

He scanned over the report a bit longer. 'Was she injured?' he asked at last.

'Don't think so.'

'Ambulance called?'

'Nah.'

'Were you on a camera bus?'

'No.'

'Any damage tae the bus?'

'Nope.'

'Did she get the bus number?'

'Doubt it.'

'Right!' he shouted and crumpled up the report and threw it in the bin. 'It didnae even happen.'

'What?'

'It didnae happen, mate. You've got nae knowledge of it.'

I just looked at him as he munched into his sausage

sandwiches. 'Look,' he said, 'if you put in that report you'll just be incriminating yourself! You'll just be admitting liability before she's even made a complaint, which, let's face it, she might never dae!'

'I'm just being honest about it,' I said.

'Dae ye know whit they dae tae honest people in here? You'll get a first and final written warnin' mate! A yellow card! Dae it again and yer oot the door!'

'But I've already told Jelly Baby about it. Wouldn't he—'

'Ach! Bugger him! He's just a desk jockey! As long as there's nothin' in writing aboot it, then yer safe.'

'What if the woman does put in a complaint?'

Driver Gollum almost spat his sausage across the canteen, 'Deny it for fuck's sake!'

I downed my coffee and went home for something stronger.

3
SOUP KITCHEN BRAWL

Meal breaks never seem to last long enough. I could still smell kebab from Driver Humpty as we stood talking at the driver changeover point. We were both moaning – me because my bus was running late, him because of stomach acid reflux. The poor chap had been suffering for days. He even said that his wife was kept awake all last night due to his burping. I felt compelled to enquire further into this and found that it was because of his uncontrollable wind. This came as a disappointment as I secretly wanted to hear that he was just triumphantly showing off to her with his gastric talents.

Baritone: Humpty burps out the finale of 'Nessun Dorma' to his poor, suffering wife. Incidentally, 'Nessun Dorma' means 'Nobody Sleeps' which fits nicely.

'It's probably because of all that crap they sell in the depot canteen,' I said.

'Oh, don't let Chowder Chops hear you say that. He makes the chips extra greasy and the curry extra dry just for me,' said Humpty.

'I'll stay away from Chowder Chops, thanks. I don't fancy having to clean my insides out with engine degreaser.'

'I should maybe give that a try. Anyway, how you findin' the rest of the job so far?' asked Humpty as a bus pulled in to the stop.

'Well, I haven't killed anyone yet,' I said. 'But I was wondering about something.'

'What's that?'

'See all those dimples in the body panels of that bus?' I said, and pointed out the pock-marks that looked as though someone had repeatedly spiked the bus with a giant tooth-pick. 'What actually causes all that?'

Humpty gave a loud belly laugh. 'They are what you might call impact craters. Made by bricks and bottles and whatever is lying around for the neds to throw at you.'

'But the bus is covered in them! Oh my God! What about the windows, they're made of glass!'

Humpty's belly laugh was even louder than before.

'We should have crash helmets as part of the uniform!'

'Aye, a few people have been injured over the years. You heading up the Drum tonight?' asked Humpty.

'Drumchapel? Yes, that's where I'm off to next.'

'Well, you never know. You might get lucky.'

I wasn't entirely sure what he meant but, as we chatted, a little pensioner at the bus stop spotted us. 'You bus drivers?' she asked.

'Yes, we are bus drivers,' I said.

'Shoot the bloody lot of you!' she spat. Yes, it seems that drivers are just as much targets for abuse as the vehicles they drive.

Fortunately, just as the little muppet started on the company's 'stupid timetables' and bus drivers' 'ridiculous driving', my bus appeared round the corner. It was being driven by Driver Weepingclown. I called him this due to the fact that he was always laughing, but he's got a scar near his right eye that looks a bit like a tear. Strangely, he was not wearing his usual grinny face just then. I wondered why – after all, the bus was nice and quiet for an evening rush hour. That had to count for something.

Weepingclown stepped out the cab and just as I was climbing aboard he said: 'Wait a minute. Got a wee problem with a punter.' He walked up the bus and I saw him talking to a dishevelled wraith whose head was bobbing from side to side. 'Don't worry mate,' said Weepingclown, 'the ambulance is on it's way.'

It was at this point that I noticed that the wretched man's face had blood streaming down one side. I reckoned there had been fisticuffs and Driver Weepingclown had contacted Control for an ambulance. Now that is real service to the community.

However, at the mention of an ambulance the man immediately stood up struggling and shouting: 'No! No ambulance! Fuck off!'

There's gratitude for you. Whatever happened, this down-and-out obviously had some good reason to avoid the authorities.

'Sit down, mate. It's already on its way.'

'You can't keep me! You can't keep me on the bus,' he shouted as he shuffled towards the exit. I instinctively stepped aside to let him pass.

But it was too late. Two cops had arrived in the meantime and were blocking the exit like two big wardrobes. 'Sit down, buddy,' said one of them. And sit down he did.

After transferring the remaining passengers to another bus, four more police arrived from Partick police station, including the Inspector (wasn't the bum honoured?) as well as an ambulance crew. A brief interrogation of Mr Bleedyhead revealed that he had had a fight with another bum in a city centre soup kitchen before running away and sneaking on the bus. He had apparently sat there groaning in front of no less than twenty passengers with blood dripping from his face and no one had told the driver. Each punter on that bus must have just crapped themselves and frozen.

Despite the man's obvious discomfort, I thought it astonishing that so many resources were being consumed by the indiscretions of a couple of Glasgow's underclass. Six police officers (not forgetting the Inspector) and an ambulance crew – all summoned because a pair of bums had an argument in a soup kitchen about probably nothing more substantial than who got more croutons. Now the bus was effectively out of service and a load of fare-paying passengers were inconvenienced.

After Mr Bleedyhead was eventually removed, it took me several hours of pedal to the metal to get the bus back on its schedule and I didn't have time for a proper break until just before my last run. And I was hoping I could get the bus through Drumchapel without being bricked.

Amazingly, we arrived at the Drumchapel terminus without a single attempt on my windows (eat that, Humpty!) and I

To people who run soup kitchens:
Please share croutons evenly amongst bums, us bus drivers
have got timetables to keep to!

switched the engine off and got out for a breather. All was dark and unusually quiet. No distant screams, shrieks or dogs barking. Strangely, the dead calm made for an even more eerie atmosphere. I could feel it in my water as I piddled up against my back tyre. Yes, something afoot was definitely in the air tonight, and it smelled fishy.

Sure enough, as I got back in the cab, the sound of a man and woman having a heated argument wafted through my cab window like that eerie funk of fish. Although they were definitely getting closer I couldn't understand every word. Nevertheless, there was no mistaking that 'fuckin'' this and 'bloody' that peppered their exchanges. This was a real Lulu.

Just as soon as my mind formed the thought, 'hope they go away and don't come near me,' God, being the perverted bastard that he is, directed their steps straight on to my bus. My prayer for a quiet night obviously didn't get through.

The chap was dressed in full ned uniform: white track suit, fake Burberry cap and dripping with gold. She was not so garish, wearing a fairly anonymous denim jacket and jeans. After a moment of calm while I printed their tickets, they sat down and immediately carried on where they had left off in the street. With the engine off I could hear that their argument centred around exactly where the ned was going to spend the night.

'I just want to come home!' girned the ned.

'Bugger off! Yer stayin' oan this bus 'till it goes into the city centre!' blasted the woman.

'Naw! I'm off it, I'm clean!'

'No yer naw, look at the state o' ye'!'

'Honest! I'll just have a couple o' joints an' that's it! I'll not even get drunk.'

'Fuck off!'

'How about I buy us both a Chinkie? I'll clean up aroun' the hoose too.'

'No! Yer stayin' oan this bus into the toon and yer goin' to the hostel.'

'Aw, no! Besides, all my stuff's up at Rab's.'

'Fuck off!'

'I just wanna come home!'

And so on. Unbelievably, fifteen minutes later they both got off at the same stop. Obviously the promise of a Chinese meal and cleaning the house won her over. Perhaps a bit cheaply, I thought. Yes, very cheaply indeed. If a junkie ned proffered me any foodstuff I would most likely deck him and make him eat it. Silly woman for taking him in. After all, what worth have the promises of a junkie?

Drove back to the depot at the end of my shift and one of the orange boiler-suited Oompa Loompas came aboard to remove the cash box. As he grovelled about, I spotted another bus parked in the yard with two upstairs windows missing.

'What happened to that bus?' I asked.

'Eh? Oh, a couple o' broken windaes,' he said casually, as though I had just asked him the time.

'Jesus! Anyone hurt?'

'Nah, don't think so. But that's the third one that's come in the night from the Drum with windaes missin'. I thought you were gonna be the fourth. It must have been party night for all the neds up there.'

'Do you think they'll catch the wee bastards that did it?'

'Well, a report usually gets sent to the polis, but, uh . . .' It was more of a sigh than an answer.

So, Humpty's simple explanation was true. Initially I thought he was just scaremongering to freak out a new driver, but it really did happen. I wondered how much crash helmets cost these days, because it was obviously going to be just a matter of time before I needed one.

4

THE MIDDLE-AGED TEENAGER

After a tough shift, I like to relax with a wee nightcap and a bit of classic soul. Tonight the warm tones of Brook Benton's 'Rainy Night In Georgia' helped me unwind, along with a glass of slightly more fiery Highland Park single malt. Unfortunately, tonight also turned out to be a rainy night in Maryhill.

I had actually been route-trained on this particular run but the streets looked very different in the soggy darkness so I was once again driving along with my nose in a map. I spied Driver Chucklemumble going in the opposite direction and gave him a wave. I could sure have done with some of his 'advithe' on how to get to the Summerston terminus. Chucklemumble's bus was surprisingly full for such a late hour and I wondered where all his punters had come from. My question was soon answered.

The bingo had just ruptured onto Maryhill Road and there were hundreds of little ball-shaped figures waddling towards the bus stops. There was no escape for any bus driver who, like me, just happened to be in the wrong place at the wrong time. I pulled into the stop, opened the doors and somehow managed to absorb dozens of twittering, cackling and spluttering pensioners. All of them were soaking wet, which had the effect of steaming up my windows and blurring the outside world even more. Glancing round at all the grey, wispy heads, it was as though they were all part of the same fluffy cumulus cloud that had somehow floated down from the sky and started to drizzle inside my bus.

Just when I thought there were no more to come, I checked my mirror only to see yet more candy floss hairstyles running in my direction. Well, when I say 'running' it was more like 'exaggerated ambling' – arms swung a bit more, lateral wobble increased and they gave a broad rictus grin – but they didn't actually move any faster. If anything, all that effort of pretending to run actually slowed them down.

After what seemed like an eternity, there was a break in the inundation and I was able to close the doors and move away. At the very next stop there was yet another old lady, but she didn't concern me as much as the younger woman with whom she was speaking. As I pulled in, I could see that the young woman was absolutely distraught. She was crying inconsolably and all her make-up had slid an inch down her face. After I opened the door, the old lady gave her a pat on the shoulder and said, 'I have to go, that's my bus.'

'Aye, I can't thank you enough, I'm so sorry about this,' sniffled the woman.

The old lady boarded the bus leaving the woman sobbing at the stop. She whispered to me, 'That lassie's got problems.'

Obviously the young woman had got talking to the old lady at the bus stop and just spilled her guts. But, despite the fact that the old lady would have been a compassionate Samaritan and offered sound advice gained through a lifetime of experience, old ladies do not come with a confidentiality clause.

Quite the opposite actually – they squeal, they squawk and they blabber. In fact, they gossip on such an industrial scale that there is no doubt that every sordid detail of that poor woman's affairs would spread at a geometric rate through Maryhill's grapevine – all thanks to one old lady. One muppet. Just one. Much tea will flow.

However, to the old lady's credit, she tried to lift the mood by complimenting a little cutesy girl who was getting off the bus with her mother. 'Look at you! Aren't you beautiful!' The little girl giggled but her mother just pulled her along, too absorbed in a mobile phone conversation to acknowledge the pensioner.

As the mother dragged her kid off the bus, I could hear what she was shouting into the phone: 'Willy's just been up tae the hoose and kicked the door in! I'm gettin' the polis tae him. He was screamin' an' shoutin' and he just booted the front door right in!'

Must have been a big Willy.

Miraculously, I managed to navigate to the terminus with only one wrong turn. I wasn't sure if I had missed the junction for Summerston, but twenty voices shouting 'Driver! You've gone the wrong way!' was a bit of a clue. There was a roundabout ahead so it was just a case of doing a U-turn and getting back on route. The bingo crowd thought it was all very funny, bless them.

After unloading my last passenger, I got to the terminus and switched the engine off. I couldn't help but feel sympathy for the sobbing woman at the bus stop and the mother with the kid whose front door was kicked in by Willy. It all smacked of violent domestic breakdown. Driving through the less affluent areas of Glasgow every day was a real eye-opener. Their plight, along with the stress of being thrown in at the deep end with my new job, was really beginning to take its toll on me. The only way I could deal with it,

God help me, was to poke fun at it. As Granny used to say, 'If ye didnae laugh, ye'd greet!'

After my brief respite at the terminus, I headed back into town. Unfortunately, the rain had done little to keep away the drunken yobbery that blights the city centre at night, and eventually I picked up four drunken buffoons. Really not what I needed just then.

They were of Eastern European origin by their accents. The tallest guy was the most frightening. To give you an idea – sometimes you see news stories where the newsreader says something like: 'and the perpetrator of these brutal murders was none other than convicted felon, Mr Knuckles Grimfist' and they flash up a picture of a swarthy, overweight, tattooed skinhead. Well, this was he.

From the moment he got on he started stamping his feet and shouting: 'Polska! (clap,clap) Polska! (clap,clap) Lo! Lo! Lo! Yeah! Driver, light is green! Good! Faster! Faster! Faster! Go! Go! Go! Polska! (clap, clap) Polska! (clap, clap) Lo! Lo! Lo!' Other punters were grinning so I just tolerated it. The cherry on the cake was when a silly little muppet wearing a yellow cagoule turned round to them and asked, 'And what nationality are you?' That just set him off again.

By Central Station the Polskas had left and all was quiet once again. Until, that is, a middle-aged woman got on with a young girl and asked for a half fare. Up until now, I never had the balls to question anyone about their age, but I was now tired, emotionally drained and felt pretty cranky.

'I want a half fare. I'm fifteen.'

'You've got to be kidding!' I said.

'I am fifteen. You think I'm lying but I'm not,' she said indignantly.

'Fifteen? Aye, fifty more like! You've even come on the bus with a cigarette!'

'Aye, so? Never seen a fifteen year old with a fag?'

'Listen, get your fare paid. The full fare.'

'I'm fifteen!'

Strangely, I found myself wavering. Not because I believed she was fifteen, but because I was driving the last bus and didn't really want to scupper the kid just because her mother was a fare-dodging kook.

Just as she was about to go really nuts, the little muppet wearing the yellow cagoule came down the bus and said, 'Don't worry, dear, I'll pay the extra,' and she plopped the required coins into the slot.

So my first 'run-in' with a punter ended in stalemate. Without thanking the muppet or even waiting for her ticket to be printed she yanked the girl up the bus and sat down. As she went, I noticed that the woman's head was a strange shape. Mainly because it didn't really have a shape. It was oddly concave and seemed to be made up of many smaller amorphous blobs that were arranged into a large compound mass. A bit like a clump of frog spawn with two eyes and a mouth. Quite unsettling.

As I was running a bit early I decided to wait for a couple of minutes at Central Station. During that time, the woman's kid got bored and started running up and down the stairs of the decker. This clearly irritated her.

'Get doon them bloody stairs ya wee bastard!' she shouted. The rest of the bus was shocked into silence. Miraculously the girl was not fazed in the slightest, probably having been desensitized to swearing at home. If my Mum said that to me at that age I would have probably wet myself and burst into tears.

'Get doon them stairs or I'll come up there and break yer neck!'

For me, that was going beyond the limits. Ironically, it is crazies like that who lead vigilante attacks against people who they suspect of being child abusers. And even that is usually only on the strength of drunken pub gossip.

Anyway, I was surprised to find myself fighting the urge to get out my cab and be the vigilante myself but, even if I did, what could I do?

'Mum, Kirsty's mum is taking her to Helensburgh. Can we go to Helensburgh?' asked the young girl as she slid down the stairs on her arse.

'Hannah, you can go where the fuck you like,' growled her mother.

Again, it was like water off a duck's back to the girl, but for me it was like the Rubicon had been crossed. You can't talk to your kids like that and expect them to grow up as balanced individuals. I was almost biting the steering wheel trying to control myself. But if I got out my cab, what would I say?

Maybe a story with a strong moral overtone might have helped. Yes, an allegory from history where someone abused a close family member and it all ended in heartbreak. How about this:

Ahem! Excuse me! Did you know that King Khufu from ancient Egypt actually made his own daughter work in a brothel in order to help fund the building of the Great Pyramid at Giza? We can't say exactly how much one of those big pyramid blocks costs but one thing is certain: Khufu's daughter must have been very busy in order to pay for a whole damned pyramid! Now you think about that every time you go to hit your kid.

There. Educational and with strong moral overtones.

THE BLOODBUS

Then again, maybe that's not the best example. It was probably as well that I just stayed put in my cab. After all, righting wrongs wasn't my job. It's the job of the police, social services and Jerry Springer. I've got a timetable to keep to.

5
YOUNG TEAM NO. 1

Before heading out to the Partick relief point, I briefly popped into the depot to see what shift I had been allocated for the following day. Just as I found my name and duty number on the noticeboard, I heard a voice from behind the desk: 'Hey, driver! You're a wanted man!'

Turning round, I saw Jelly Baby wearing an evil grin. 'That's him there,' he said, nodding towards a man standing next to him. A man I'd never seen before. A man wearing a smart suit. A man who was clean shaven. Damn, must be a manager.

'A quick word with you, driver,' said The Manager, and motioned me to step through to his office.

As I walked through and sat down, there was no doubt in my mind what this was going to be about. I knew that my wee elbow doink on Renfield Street a couple of weeks ago was going to come back and bite me. Hard. Why didn't I just own up to it at the time?

The Manager clicked away on his computer for a while before shuffling through some papers on his desk. I saw my name at the top of one of the pages with COMPLAINT stamped beside it in large letters. I prepared for the worst.

'We've received a telephone complaint from a woman regarding an incident one week ago last Thursday.' He paused and looked at me. 'Do you know yourself what it might be about?'

'Um, erm, well . . .' I mumbled, with dry mouth and sweaty

palms. Just as I was about to spill my guts about the guts I had spilled, I remembered why I hadn't come clean about it before. *Dae ye know whit they dae tae honest people in here?* were Driver Gollum's exact words. No, I didn't know, and I didn't want to find out today. So I feigned ignorance. 'Absolutely no idea at all.'

He picked up the page and studied it. 'The complaint is from an elderly woman who said she was standing on Dalmarnock Road with her elderly male companion.'

Eh? That did not sound like Miss Rabbit Ears.

He continued: 'She said, "I held out my walking stick in full view of the bus, but even though I made eye contact with the bus driver, the bus just sped up and drove right past. It was the last bus and I had to pay a ten pound taxi fare to get home. Will I be reimbursed?"'

This was a total surprise to me and, in a way, a relief. Accidentally driving past a punter was not even in the same ballpark as whacking someone with the front of your bus. Even though I had absolutely no recollection of anyone holding out their walking stick at me on Dalmarnock Road, I actually unclenched a little bit and relaxed. 'Oh, I didn't even realise. Sorry about that. I must have just, erm . . . I'm not long in the job, you see.'

'I can see that from your record,' he said and put down the piece of paper. 'But I'm afraid it's a bit more serious because you were the last bus and she had to pay for a taxi home. Because of that, I can't just give you a verbal, it will have to be formal disciplinary action.' He fumbled about on his desk with more pieces of paper. Surely he hadn't typed up the first and final already?

As he sifted through the papers, something didn't quite sit right in my mind. Why didn't I have any recollection of this event? I would definitely have remembered a pensioner holding out her walking stick at me because many pensioners did that and it really bugged me.

'Not the best start to your bus driving career,' said The Manager. 'It'll stay on your record for —'

'Wait a minute,' I said. 'When did you say this happened?'

'A week ago last Thursday.'

I fished out my diary and thumbed through to that day. 'That was my day off!'

'Eh?' said The Manager and gave me a sideways look before turning round and clicking his computer keyboard.

'I wasn't even working that day! You've got the wrong man!'

He fiddled with his computer for what seemed like an hour. 'Oh, true enough,' he said eventually. 'My apologies.' He took the piece of paper off his desk, crumpled it up into a tiny ball and threw it in the bin. 'I'll see that the relevant people get their knuckles rapped for that.'

I left the room and walked past the main depot office. 'Still in a job?' shouted Jelly Baby, sneering. I ignored him my mind was still swimming.

Oh, my God! I may have been a loose cannon behind the wheel, but a loose cannon behind a desk was equally deadly. What if I had just sat there and accepted it? What if I had come right out and admitted the elbow doink? Either way I would now be on a yellow card and only one foul away from an early bath. I decided to walk to the driver relief point at Partick to clear my head. It was over a mile away but a little exercise usually calms me down. I'd only got a few hundred yards when a taxi screeched to the side of the road and gave a long blast of the horn.

'Hey, pal!' shouted the scowling lump of a driver. 'One of your buses knocked a wing mirror off my car!'

'Oh?' I said, quite taken aback after my little chat with The Manager. 'Which bus?'

'Dunno, but I'm bloody furious!' and he bared his teeth to show that he most certainly was. 'They all come down my street hitting parked cars. Don't you have to pass a test to drive those bloody things?'

Well, this was just great. It seemed that just wearing a bus driver's uniform in the street can attract a bizarre array of freakery from the public. 'When did it happen?' I asked, trying to calm him down.

'A few weeks ago. Last month, or something.'

Last month for Christ's sake! Well, I almost made free with an oath. One driver takes his wing mirror off and suddenly all bus drivers are scoundrels. Now that's what I call resentment. Still, I suppose some British war veterans dislike the entire Japanese race for their treatment of allied POWs. However, witnessing your compatriots being vivisectioned and boiled alive is probably more grounds for a life-long grudge than having a wing mirror knocked off your car.

Spooked: Crabby cabbie goes crazy.

After the cabbie vented his spleen for a few more minutes I informed him that the correct course of action was to write a letter to the company. However, I could sense that the oaf would probably have to get someone else to write it for him, what with him having nothing more than rice pudding for brains.

He wasn't too concerned with my advice and simply mounted another expletive-rich invective against bus drivers. He was howling, spitting and waving his arms around in a malevolent mardi gras. Us lot obviously disturb him very powerfully. Sneaking up on this guy, even in several decades time, and shouting 'Bus!' would probably achieve the same complete constitutional failure as sneaking up on a war veteran today and shouting 'Sushi!'

At last, the cabbie made off and I continued on my way to Partick. Now, at the relief point, I picked up a rather busy bus from Driver Stingball, but managed to avoid much of his biting sarcasm and poker-faced put downs. Definitely one of the biggest mouths in the depot. It was just as well I knew the bus route up to Knightswood. I didn't fancy the idea of asking Stingball for directions. He would no doubt take full advantage of the situation, then brag to everyone in the Partick bothy that he had sent a new driver to Loch Lomond.

As I headed up Crow Road my bus radio crackled into life:

Incoming Radio Message: *Central Control to all services in the Byres Road area. This is a missing person enquiry on behalf of the police. We're looking for an elderly male, five foot nine, grey hair, wearing brown trousers, a brown waistcoat, a cream sweater and flip flops.*

Ha ha! Flip flops! Not exactly going to be difficult to spot wearing those. Mind you, there is a University up there and I have seen various academic professor types going about dressed like grand patriarchs of some wacky New Age commune. The Age of Aquarius has most certainly dawned on Byres Road. The fugitive was no doubt strategically blending in amongst them. Good thinking.

Thankfully, by the time I reached Knightswood the bus was a lot lighter. This was good because it meant there were less people to suffer injury from projectiles if the Knightswood Young Team were on the prowl. Usually they were, and tonight was no exception.

I could see about twelve youths standing in the middle of the road up ahead and it was clear they had spotted me. There was nothing I could have done. You can't just say, 'Excuse me ladies and gentlemen, does anyone know a detour that will get me round these bloodthirsty delinquents?' I had to follow the bus route and that took me straight into the jaws of the Young Team.

They stood in the middle of the road blocking my way, so I slowed to walking pace. That's when I noticed the nedette swinging the cricket bat. I couldn't believe it! A girl was going to make an attempt on my windows with a damned cricket bat! I heard the KYT usually prefer airborne ordinance such as stones and bottles, but this was the first attack I had heard of using sports equipment.

She walked calmly round to the side of the bus and took a hefty swing. The sound of willow on glass made more of a *bong* than a *crash*, but to my amazement the window remained intact. Mind you, the sudden loud impact made a little muppet on the bus go 'Whoop!'

The nedette squared up again. Hoisting the bat even

higher, she took an even bigger swing. But again, bong rather than crash. The bus was beginning to edge away from her at this point, so she took one final, frustrated swing. But for a third time, the window denied her.

Her complete failure to even make a scratch gave me a sort of malignant satisfaction. For any self-respecting Young Team, a debauched night of ultra-violence was not complete without the tinkle of bus glass on tarmac. Otherwise how could they justify writing KYT No. 1 everywhere? More like No. 5 or No. 6 if you ask me.

Denied: Final Score - KYT All Out for zero.

After an embarrassing cock-up such as this, the KYT would no doubt be eclipsed in the Young Team Delinquency League by not only the Young Posso Fleeto, Young Parkhead Rebels and Young Scotstoun Fleet, but even those jocular types who call themselves the Yoker Krazy Krew – the ignominy!

There was no point in contacting the Control Room. In one of his explosive rants in the canteen, Driver Gollum had informed me that unless two or three buses in a row got their windows smashed, they wouldn't even bother sending a police car round, or even condescend to put out a radio call for the benefit of other buses. Damn it, the Young Team knew it and all of them wore a smirk as I zoomed round the corner to get away.

Finally, I reached the terminus, switched the engine off and tried to catch my breath. A hobbly old lady standing at the stop tapped the door, 'Ven are you leaving, driver?'

That was a German accent I was detecting. 'Five minutes,' I said. 'Hop on and take a seat.'

'Dank you.'

I thought it only right to warn her about the KYT death squad that were going about tonight and she seemed suitably disgusted. Then, as bus muppets often do, she began telling me a story: 'I vill tell you vot I saw on ze news.'

Hang on, let me strap in.

'A man on a bus in London kept throwing heez feesh and cheeps at another man's goorlfirend. Ze other man told heem to stop, but he deedn't stop. He kept throwing heez feesh and cheeps at heez goorlfriend. Zen, you know vot heppened?'

Do I know what happened? Well, let's see. Based on what I'd heard around the depot campfire, people often start shouting and swearing at each other, then they start the spitting, and finally they end up rolling around the floor of the bus in a drunken brawl amongst the empty beer cans and fast food leavings. Then, unless one of them pulls out a knife, the fight fizzles out as one of them flees the bus. But I was interested to hear what she had to say, so I let her continue.

'He moordoored heem!' she exclaimed.

So, one of them did pull out a knife then. Ahh, the things people do just to keep their Young Team ahead of the Yoker Krazy Krew in the Young Team Delinquency League.

If I came across the KYT again on the return leg, I had decided not to slow down like I did before. Even if a dozen old ladies were standing at the bus stop waving their walking sticks in the air, I'd rather take my chances with The Manager once again than give those retards a chance to make up for lost vandalism.

6
PIRATE'S TREASURE

Remember when you were a kid and you went down to the seashore? Ahh yes, the raw sewage and washed-up condoms – sheer bliss. But you may also remember curiously turning over large rocks only to find crawly, jumpy gnats underneath that made you scream and run away. Well, I was discovering that Glasgow was a bit like that too. Take a look under the city's bloated underbelly by hopping on a bus at night and you will find the human equivalent of those crawly, jumpy gnats. The only difference is that on a bus you can't run away.

It was the evening rush hour and, like a big lint roller, I trundled through the city streets picking up all manner of flotsam and jetsam on the ebb tide. On Bath Street I was flagged down by a swarthy, boozed-up pirate whose spinnaker was a long, grey coat that sported more holes than a tea bag. If you held the garment up to the light it would be a veritable planetarium of constellations. But maybe that was the intention – each hole representing a star, a perfect replica of the night sky for navigating home from the pub.

'D'ye go tae Clydebank?' he slurred.

'I think so,' I said without much conviction. By now I knew most routes in the depot but, unfortunately, not this one. I hadn't bothered to go out and learn it in my car, thinking it would probably never come up, but it was just like Jelly Baby to throw me a curve ball. My nose was once again buried in maps.

The sozzled seaman took absolutely ages to hoist himself on to the bus using his one practicable leg, and even longer to painstakingly search the contents of each pocket for his bus pass. Eventually he found it and presented it to me with a toothy grin. I don't know what he was smiling about because the pass was several millennia out of date. I steeled myself for an ejection.

But before I could give him his orders to walk the plank, he thrust a fist full of sweets through my cab door. 'Dat's for you, driver,' he said. What's this? Could this marooned old wino be entreating me to accept a bribe of half a dozen sweets in return for travel privileges? Naturally I accepted and let him board. After all, he was stinking of booze and urine and I didn't want to get my hands dirty throwing him off.

However, two tubby munchkins wearing cleaner's tabards were all this time queuing behind the Pirate and growing more impatient with the delay. 'We're tryin' to get on the bus, for Christ's sake!' said the more rotund of the two.

Attack of the Munchkins: Their appearance and deportment suggested that in their youth they skipped school on the day that teacher explained the differences between 'erogenous' and 'androgynous'.

The Pirate half turned and mumbled something as he shuffled up the bus, as though cursing them to a parrot on his shoulder. As we moved off, I could hear the Munchkins progress from maligning the Pirate to maligning, well, pretty much everything else:

'Oh, God! It's a smelly bus! I just wanna go home.'

'Me too. Remember I used to live in the Gorbals?'

'Aye, you didn't like it there.'

'I hated it. Too many Irish.'

'Aye. You've got a nice hoose now, though.'

'Aye, but only when I'm on the late shift. See when I'm on the late shift, my hoose is spotless. Spotless! Then he comes in from work and I say to him "Take yer boots aff afore ye walk across ma good floor!" and he says "What is this a fuckin mosque?"'

'Cheeky bastard!'

Most women harbour a compulsive cleaning instinct but I've noticed that amongst the lower echelons, this instinct is more of a pathological obsession. It's just a pity that for all their polishing, scrubbing, dusting and vacuuming, what comes out of their mouths is often more repugnant than even the most bepubed plughole.

I was now so late that the bus running fifteen minutes behind me had caught up. It was being driven by Driver Stingball and he seemed quite content to just sit behind me and let me do all the work, even though my bus was standing room only. 'You wait bloody ages and then two come along at once!' was all I got through Hyndland. Still, Stingball did not overtake and lend a hand. Bastard!

Fortunately, the Munchkins and the Pirate behaved themselves for the rest of the journey, which surprised me.

The same could not be said for the fellow who formed the subject of the next radio announcement:

> Incoming Radio Message: *This is Central Control to all services in the Easterhouse area. Beware of a man trying to board with an invalid ticket at Easterhouse shopping centre. He's got a dog with him and if you challenge him about the ticket he sets the dog on you.*

That was definitely going to give me nightmares.

Having now unloaded all of my cargo, I got to the Clydebank terminus and took the number of Stingball's bus as he pulled in to the terminus behind me. Screw me, will you? We'll see.

Then I set about those sugary bribes that the Pirate gave me. I was actually feeling quite good about myself in that I had maintained good control over the bus all the way here despite three inches of play in the steering and brakes that I had to really stand on. As I plopped the first sweet in my mouth, I considered that if I had been given this bus on my very first shift, I'd probably have taken down a lot more than just a wheelie bin.

Wait a minute. Liqourice alert! Aargh! Damn it! I hate liqourice!

I hate any food that I don't understand and I don't understand liqourice! In a reflex action I spat the offending sweet out the window. What the hell is liqourice? What is it made out of? Based on taste and texture I would have to say old bus tyres. And what's the deal with that Bertie Basset, the crazy liqourice candy clown? Personally, I think Bertie Basset is just the Michelin Man with an extra chromosome. The rest of the sweets went out the window very quickly too. Never, ever, take bribes from a tramp!

At the end of my shift I signed off in the depot office and told Jelly Baby about being tailed all the way to Clydebank by Stingball. He just laughed. 'It's what you call "getting shafted". He probably knew you were a new start and thought you wouldn't tipple.'

'Aye, well I did tipple. I was getting grief from all the punters for being late and he just sat there behind me, letting me do all the work.'

'That's exactly why he sat behind you, he didn't want all the grief.'

'Here's his bus number,' and I handed over the piece of paper.

'Ach! Stop being such a cry baby! It happens to everyone when they're new. You get shafted. That's all there is too it.'

'Oh, thanks very much for your concern!'

'Don't worry, when you've been in the job a while it'll be you shafting the new starts. You'll be the pumper instead of the pumpee.' Jelly Baby grinned.

'Who's pumping new starts?' asked a bearded and bespectacled driver as he came into the depot office to sign off. It was Driver Kisses. He looked me up and down and said, 'That's my job.'

'I'll just leave it for now,' I said, and beat a very hasty retreat from the depot.

7

GOLLUM'S FUNERAL

'Bitch!' cursed Driver Ubu and threw down a paper bag containing a bread roll on to the table.

I was eating a Pot Noodle in the Partick bothy, a grubby wee hidey hole with a few tables and chairs and a portable TV where drivers take their break. It was a miserable, bleak, windowless den, completely devoid of any comfort or cheer and was situated very appropriately next to an undertaker. Even the skankiest hooker would probably prefer you did her up a close or behind a garage than in this grim little hovel.

'I asked her for a soft roll, but the bitch in the shop gave us a bloody crispy roll,' moaned Ubu. He eyed the offending roll with grave suspicion, as though it were about to leap out of the bag and snap at his nose. Ending up with a crispy roll instead of a soft roll might not herald the end of the world to you or I, but to someone like Driver Ubu, who wears dentures, it was a full-on crisis. All eyes were upon him as he tentatively nibbled at the well-baked bread. He chewed slowly and finally swallowed. He nodded to everyone in the bothy to signify that he was okay.

Then, another nibble, another chew and another swallow, and again everything seemed fine. But on his third chew, his face suddenly became anguished and hideously contorted. Throwing down the roll, he hastily yanked the top row of false teeth out of his head and furiously lapped off all the bits of crust that had got behind his dentures.

My Pot Noodle and I just looked at each other.

'Shee what dat bitch hash done tae me!' bellowed a toothless and rueful Ubu. 'Dat'sh why I ashk her for a fuckin' shoft roll!'

Having slurped up the last irritating crumbs with his tongue he shoved his teeth back into his head with a delightful clop that sounded like a golf ball rattling into the hole. But before he could take another reluctant bite, the door to the bothy was flung asunder.

There, silhouetted against the light, was the unmistakable figure of Driver Gollum. A tall, gangly driver is he, whose capacity for foul language and ridicule is matched only by his appetite for tobacco leaf and beer.

But even then, I hoped he might behave himself because there was a funeral party assembling outside the undertaker's next door. Surely he would show some respect for a funeral. Unfortunately, Gollum was off duty and had spent most of the day drinking in the Hayburn Vaults pub. Now, all liquored up and glazed, he decided to storm the bothy at FULL volume to tell us how great it was that we had to work and he didn't.

'HA! HA! HA! Look at you all! You're all workin' and I'm no! Ya bunch o' dour-faced bastards!' he hollered. 'Look at him! His heid's doon! (point) His heid's doon! (point) And his heid's doon! (point) You're all a bunch o' glum bastards!'

Yes, but probably not as glum as the party of mourners who were standing within earshot of this human wrecking ball.

'Crisps! Right noo!' yelled Gollum. With an attack of the munchies, he turned his attention to the vending machine. After plopping in some change, he typed in the code for a packet of Quavers. However, sometimes the machine doesn't dislodge the snack properly and it gets stuck on the shelf instead of dropping down to the collection tray below.

'AW! NO!' blasted Gollum as his packet of crisps refused to fall. He took to thumping the machine with his fists and rocking it back and forth. 'Gimme ma bloody crisps!' he yelled and tilted the machine backwards until it smacked the wall, nearly putting a hole in the plasterboard between the bothy and the undertakers. A definite distraction if you were paying your last respects to the departed next door.

Precious Quavers: It's ours it is! And we wants it!

'Gimme ma Quavers ya' money grabbing bastard!' thrashed Gollum with greater vigour. With a schlump, the crisps eventually fell down into the collection tray. 'YES!' belted Gollum, 'Right, I'm away to put a line oan. Yous can all get tae fuck!' And with that, he stumbled out of the bothy.

A strange calm descended over the remaining drivers after Gollum left. That sort of 'restoration of reality' calm that made us look at each other as if to say, 'Did that really just happen? Or did we just imagine it?' Maybe the wind just whipped up the rubbish that was blowing around the street into human form, blew it inside the bothy and made moaning noises that sounded like words. Maybe if we looked outside, there would just be a mound of filth and garbage on the ground, like a snowman just leaves a carrot and a puddle.

'Worsht thing aboot it,' started Driver Ubu, who was once again lapping at his dentures, 'he beginsh hish shift th' morra mornin' at five o'clock. Imagine being a punter on hish bush?' (clop)

Shortly after this, a sign was pinned to the bothy door saying: 'Please show respect when a funeral is in progress.'

8

THE LOVE BRICK

Saturday nights in Glasgow are an excuse for the peasant class to throw off the customary restraints of law and morality and vent forth their darker passions in a drunken orgy of felonious glee. After dark, societal norms begin to break down as alcohol sets free the Devil within. I definitely did not want to be 'shafted' again tonight by other drivers and even ran a shade early to avoid being caught by the bus behind. I already had a whole back seat of Buckfast swilling neds and did not want any more, thank you. Not good for the ol' ticker. Neither are ominous radio announcements.

> Incoming Radio Message: *Central Control to all services in the Castlemilk area, do not go to the Castlemilk terminus – there is a guy at the terminus going bananas with a knife. Control out.*

Unfortunately, the bus radio volume was set rather high and the group of young neds at the back of the bus overheard the announcement. 'Ha, ha, ha! Did you hear that, Stevie? A guy goin' bananas with a knife in Castlemilk! Pure quality!' He took another pull at his Buckfast before saying: 'That'll be wee Brian's mob. He's pure nuts! C'mon we'll go up tae Castlemilk the noo!'

There, in a nutshell, is the mindset of the Ned. And yes, it probably would fit into a nutshell. To actually want to venture in the direction of a knife-wielding maniac is beyond the wildest hypotheses of even the most fanciful psychologist – but it is just so ned.

At Cathkin I pulled in, having been flagged down by yet more neds. There were five inebriated females and one male cavorting at the stop. Judging by their dress, the females positively exulted in their neddery: big hoop earrings, dyed blond hair, ferocious make up, white skimpy tops and lamb shank hips that bulged out of tight, white, low-rise jeans. The style they had all gone for was not FCUK so much as BTICH.

The male, who was waiting for a different bus, was trying to hug and kiss as many of the females as he could before they boarded. The more hysterical members of the group were worked into a frenzy of screaming and whooping by this. With the females now on the bus and out of reach, the ned resorted to showing off his withered, elf-like physique to gain their favour. He ran and lolloped around the bus stop like a regular circus tumbler in a vain attempt to recapture the females' attention.

However, this did not work to his satisfaction and he received a stinging snub from the 'ladies' as they shambled up to the back of the bus. They may only have been nedettes, but I could sense they all had the measure of him. Even ned girls are put off by sad gits who just exude *I'll be thrashing myself off over the memory of kissing your cheek for weeks to come.*

Rather than accept defeat gracefully, the spurned ned decided to give his little harem a goodbye present to remember him by. As I was pulling out of the bus stop, I checked my left wing mirror and saw the ned stoop and pick something up. He creased himself up like a baseball pitcher before releasing a brick at the rear window of the bus.

Kaboom!

What a bang! Fortunately, despite being fractured, the window still hung in its frame. Good thing too, if the glass had spurted out over the fleshy she-neds there would have been much work for paramedics. Modern buses are fitted with double glazed windows which take a hefty swing to disintegrate. The skinny, undernourished ned clearly wasn't equal to the task.

However, the girly neds whooped so loudly that I'm pretty sure several factories in the area downed tools thinking it was the hooter for break time. Exactly why the ned threw the brick I don't know. Any psychoanalyst would no doubt draw comparisons with the chest-beating display of the rutting gorilla. Well, perhaps spider monkey would be more appropriate here. In any case, it was just so ned.

In the meantime, I had floored it to get away from the ned who was now just casually leaning against the bus stop. At the next stop I pulled in and put the handbrake on. Jumping out my cab, I addressed the girlie harem up the back.

'Excuse me, what was that guy's name?'

Silence.

Another passenger butted in: 'Tell him! I heard you talking about him a second ago. His name is Jamie or something. I heard them talking.'

'No it's not! We've never seen him before!' shouted the nedettes.

They were protecting his identity. I could sense that the Love Brick had elevated the ned's standing within the harem. In their eyes he was now an 'Alpha Ned'. My God, it was happening! The brick at the window was simply foreplay and one of the nedettes will no doubt offer herself to him at their next chance encounter at a bus stop. In Cathkin, a brick through your window is every bit a serenade as a Shakespearean love sonnet.

The Love Brick: Urban caveman proclaims his affection for chosen wench.

At least I had popped my cherry with my very first broken window. I had been dreading this moment since I started and, despite being rather shaken, was actually relieved now it had happened. So, what now? After being a victim of crime, surely I was to be relieved of duty for the rest of the day. Surely I would not be put back in charge of a ten ton vehicle with people on it after my ordeal. Unbelievably, Central Control just sent me back to the depot to get a replacement bus and to start in service again as soon as possible. With over 160 bus windows smashed every week in Glasgow, I suppose Management had become quite blasé about how they dealt with it. After all, it wouldn't be them having the nightmares.

9
THE SUNDAY PIT BULL

At the bus station, hundreds of raggedy pigeons were all aflap as they busied themselves with lovemaking and parasite pecking. It was quite embarrassing to watch all this debauchery when you're sitting next to a gaggle of old ladies. It felt like being forced to sit and watch cheap porn with nuns.

From around the corner came Driver Gurglegulp with my bus. Today it was an old Volvo single decker with a rotten funk of damp in the cab. Gurglegulp peeled himself out and informed me that the bus had been sitting in the depot yard all night with the cab window open and the rain had soaked the driver's seat. Smelled to me like the whole bus had thrush.

What a stench! I'm pretty sure that if I had checked under the driver's seat there would have been mushrooms growing and wood lice running around. Also, it looked every bit as bad as it smelled; brown and sludgy like Gurglegulp had farted out a pint of Guinness before he came round the corner.

I set off into the darkness sitting on six Metro newspapers to keep my backside dry, but every muppet that boarded informed me that my bus stank. Oh, really? If they could guarantee to me that their husbands wouldn't defecate on a whim and their grandchildren wouldn't vom down my gangway, then and only then could they throw stones.

At Balmore Road I picked up a Chinese woman and her young daughter and for the whole way to Springburn the little girl just sat there and said:

'Wobble wobble wobble wobble wobble wobble wobble . . .'

It was initially quite amusing but then I found myself thinking: Enough! Make it stop! I've heard of Chinese water torture but never Chinese wobble torture. Still the wobbles continued. I was getting so worked up that if her mother had club feet then I would have used one of them as a weapon to . . . to . . . Stop! Calm down.

Deep breaths, that's right. Composure. There will be no clubbing of children's heads with their mother's feet on this bus. But the little punk was adamant about her wobbles to the last.

At the end of the run I got to the terminus and shut the engine off. The other bus at the terminus was just getting ready to set off on the return leg, but before he left, I though I'd catch him and bum a spare ticket roll as I was running a bit low. I got out the cab and knocked on his door. There were a few passengers on the bus already but I couldn't quite make out who the driver was, yet I could just discern a beard and a set of spectacles. The doors swished open and I realised with horror who was sitting in the cab. It was Driver Kisses.

'D'you have a spare ticket roll?' I asked, nervously.

His hand moved furtively down and unlatched his cab door. He cocked an eye back towards his passengers. 'New driver,' he called, and ticked his head in my direction. 'I'll show you what we do with new drivers,' he said and sprung out of his cab at me like a Jack in the box with pouted lips. However, my reflexes were primed in advance and I sprinted back towards my own bus. He was quickly on my tail and chased me around the back of the vehicle before getting out of breath and giving up. 'I'm not finished with you!' he wheezed. 'I love a challenge!' I turned round and slapped my ass to tease him. He just gritted his teeth and shook his fist at me before returning to his bus. The passengers were in hysterics. Ha, ha! Not today, Kisses! I never did get that ticket roll, though.

Later on, at Edinburgh Road, I chanced upon a couple of happy drunks who wanted to go into town. They paid their fare to the penny and shuffled up the bus. I usually waited until drunks were seated before I moved off so they didn't flail around and land on someone. Even then, these guys were so drunk it was like watching Laurel and Hardy with bars of soap tied to their feet.

A couple of stops later, I was hailed by a young woman who struggled to get her pram up the steps of the bus.

'You'll need to fold the pram down before you can bring it on,' I said.

'But my daughter's asleep, I don't want to wake her up!' replied the woman.

'Just let her on with the pram, driver!' shouted drunken Laurel and Hardy from up the back.

'This bus isn't designed for prams, you'll have to fold it down and put it in the luggage rack.'

'Fuck's sake, driver!' said Laurel and Hardy who then decided to amble down the bus and help the woman on with the pram.

What should have taken ten seconds took six minutes thanks to the efforts of the drunken duo. They fell up the stairs, swore oaths and smacked the pram against handrails as they manoeuvred it on to the bus. Of course, all this woke the kid up who now began to cry. Great, that's all I needed.

'Shhhh! Sit nice, Megan, sit nice, there's a good girl!' said the woman to the shrieking kid, with absolutely no effect whatsoever.

'Where you from?' asked one of the drunks to the woman. A perfectly innocent question, but in Glasgow innocent questions can be met with far from innocent answers.

'Clydebank,' said the woman, 'but I got a flat in Easterhoose because of Megan's violent dad.'

'Oh?'

'Aye, he was physically abusive. He punched me here (point), here (point) and here (point).'

'Jesus!' said the drunk.

'That's not all. He used to grab my throat like this (grab) and I would bite his arm like this (bite). He's a total psycho! One time he threw the iron at me like this (wham) so I flung the frying pan at him, and he was like this: Aaaarrgg! Then he pulled a kitchen knife on me. The bastard went to court for that.'

There was a turgid pause as the drunks gathered their thoughts. Even through the numbing veil of alcohol intoxication they could sense this was not just idle bus chat but the fiery embers of an ominous domestic breakdown.

'Aye, you're better aff getting away from that,' ventured one of the drunks. What kind of place is this where drunks talk more sense than the sober?

'I wish I could get away from him, but I have to see him every Sunday because of Megan,' said the woman sullenly.

'Oh. Was it the court that decided that?'

'Court? No! I have to take Megan round to his house every Sunday coz she likes to ride around the backyard on his new pit bull.'

Go ride the dog, Megan. I need a quick word with your mother . . .

With that I almost crashed the bus. I was suppressing the laughter so much that I had to pull in and stop for my own safety. In a way, I was shocked that I had become so numb to another human being's pathetic plight that I had to stifle my chuckles. At any other time I would have balked at hearing a story like this, but in the frightening and merciless world I had entered, it was survival of the fittest. It was either you or them. Down here, in society's basement, you're either a pumper or a pumpee.

10

SICK

Well, tonight I decided to do a little pumping of my own. I was fed up being shafted all week by more experienced drivers, so when I noticed the bus in front of me was running late, I just sat behind him and dawdled along. Not right behind him, of course, not close enough to make it too obvious, but just a couple of minutes behind, just enough to stay out of his wing mirrors and let him do all the work. If I timed it just right, he wouldn't even know I was here. I hoped it was Driver Stingball. Ahh, my revenge would be so sweet.

Wrong.

Turned right at Bridgeton Cross and there was the bus, sitting with his hazard warning lights on blocking the whole road. I pulled up behind him and stopped. Immediately, the driver got out his cab and marched like a man possessed towards my bus. It was Driver Gollum, of all people. I watched in disbelief as he pulled out my windscreen wipers, knocked both my wing mirrors out of line, opened the emergency door at the back of my bus and lifted the engine flap. My dash console lit up with alarms and warning lights. 'Now, don't fuckin' tail me again! Right?' he shouted and walked away. He had just given me the bus equivalent of a wedgy.

I should really have known better. Drivers have to develop a sixth sense about being shafted because I was sure he hadn't actually seen me crawling along behind him. They can probably sense a shafter like a dolphin senses a shark. But why the hell did it have to be Gollum? At least now I knew what to do when Driver Stingball tried it on with me again. Bus wedgies leave you feeling quite violated.

My troubles weren't over yet, though. After I closed everything that Gollum had opened and had fixed my wing mirrors, I returned to the cab to hear the most unsettling noises coming from upstairs.

'Gwuuuughrrgghh! (spit) (spit),' then, 'Yuuuyynnggh! (spit).'

A little grey muppet came down the bus and said: 'Driver, I think someone might have just been sick up the back of the top deck!'

You think? Where's the doubt? An ale-washed bum got on ten minutes ago, his empty bottle has been rattling around the floor every time the bus went around a corner, he just made yakking, retching noises and now the whole bus was filled with the hideous funk of bile – and you think he might have been sick? Do you think it's even remotely possible that he just had a really bad sneeze or something? Silly muppet.

I radioed the Control Room to let them know I had a soiled bus and was hopeful they would send me back to the depot to get a replacement. No such luck. The controller said, 'Just block off the stairs to the upper deck and continue in service only using the lower deck.'

'Block the stairs with what?' I asked.

'Just use your imagination.'

Well that was helpful. As a last resort I switched off the upstairs lights and roped the stairs off with six feet of ticket roll that I ejected from the ticket machine and tied around the handrails. A flimsy barrier, but it seemed to deter passengers from going upstairs for the most part. Most normal passengers that is. Until, of course, the neds got on.

At East Kilbride bus station two freaky neds quirked on to

the bus, and where do neds always sit? That's right – upstairs at the very back. So as they boarded, I shouted after them to stay downstairs, but with a flick of their wrist they showed me their middle finger, marched through the flimsy paper cordon that I had fashioned and went straight up to vom city.

Have it your way, I thought. I made no further attempt to stop them going upstairs, smug in the knowledge of what lay in wait for them in the dark . . .

I kept the upstairs lights off so they couldn't see the surprise and as soon as I heard the little runts clumping up the gangway to the rear of the top deck I hit the gas; and sure enough they both met their slippery doom: wump and wump. They went down on top of each other like two sacks of spuds.

'Whoa! What da fuck is dat?' I heard them shriek in the dark as they floundered in warm bile. The puke must have been extra viscous and stuck to their Nikes because they found it quite a business to right themselves. Mind you, my deliberately erratic driving was doing them no favours either. *That* is for every window you've smashed with a bottle. *That* is for every seat you've slashed with a blade and *that* is for every ceiling you've graffittied with a marker pen.

Roll With It: Just as well their track suits were so garishly coloured the puke might not show up too much.

SICK

Unfortunately it was too dark to see them rolling around on my CCTV screen, but then again, sometimes imagination is better than experience. I did actually feel sorry for the person who had to clean it all up back at the depot. Over the last couple of months, I've returned to the depot with some seriously soiled buses: beer, piss, puke, broken glass, fast food leavings, chewing gum on seats, marker pen up the walls and even blood on the floor. Those depot Oompa Loompas must have nerves of steel.

11

I'LL SHOW YOU MY PUDDING!

Having foolishly forgotten to pack my sandwiches, I was forced to venture into the depot canteen and purchase something from Chowder Chops and his greasy slop shop. I asked for haggis and mash which was duly scooped onto my plate. There were no forks in the cutlery tray, so Chowder Chops ducked beneath the counter to find one. His belly must have got in the way at some point because he stumbled and dropped the fork on the ground. Without a thought, he picked it up, wiped it on his greasy apron and placed it on my plate.

'How about a clean fork?' I asked.

'That fork is clean – you just watched me clean it, didn't you?' said Chowder Chops.

'Well, I watched you wipe it on your apron.'

'Look, mate, that fork's just oot the bloody dishwasher.'

'I don't care, it was on the ground and I want a different one!'

'Tryin' to say I've got a grubby floor?'

'It's the grubby apron I'm worried about.'

'At least workin' in here I've got an excuse for havin' a grubby apron. Half o' you drivers don't look like you've seen a bar o' soap in months.'

'Hey! That was uncalled for!'

Driver Guy Smiley was next in the queue and grew impatient. 'Would you two just kiss and make up? I want my dinner!'

'Someone talking about kisses?' shouted a bearded and bespectacled driver on the other side of the canteen.

'Fair enough,' I said. 'I'll just use a teaspoon.' And so I sat in the canteen and ate my haggis and mash with a bloody teaspoon. To Chowder Chops' credit, it did taste quite nice and was very filling. Especially useful when you've get a five-hour stretch on an East Kilbride run to get through.

So, there I was, driving up Hope Street, happily digesting my haggis and mash when:

Incoming Radio Message: *Central Control to all services on Great Western Road at Blairdardie. Watch out for a group of about ten youths in the area. They're flagging down buses and when you're stopped at the bus stop they try to put fireworks down your fuel tank. Control out.*

It was probably the Knightswood Young Team trying to score points in the Young Team Delinquency League. If they couldn't take out a bus with a cricket bat, then they'd damn well blow one up instead. There is NO way I would be stopping in Blairdardie tonight! Not for anyone. Even if it's a gaggle of twittering old muppets waving their walking sticks at me to make me stop, I would just shake my head and roll past.

My thoughts were fraught with such terrible imaginings that I almost didn't notice the young drunkard who was taking ages to fish some coins out of his pocket.

'I'm going to Scotstoun, driver,' he said at last.

'Are you? I'm not,' I said and watched him try to take a bite out of his black pudding. Ahh, pig's blood in batter. It's amazing what people are willing to eat when they're in that pissed-n-hungry state. Mind you, he was so drunk that he couldn't actually bite through it, he just stuck it in his mouth and sort of *fellated* it.

'Right,' he said. 'I'll just get you along to Partick and then I'll jump on a number 62 to Scotstoun.'

Fair enough. He paid his fare and walked up the bus. You might think that the act of sitting down was fairly straight forward, even when you're drunk, but this guy took three separate attempts to affix his rear to a seat without falling over.

(Crackle, crackle – beep) Oh shit, that'll be the radio. Here we go again . . .

Incoming Radio Message: *Central Control to all Motherwell services; beware of a large group of children in the Craigneuk area. When you stop at the traffic lights they sneak up to the side of the bus and smash your windows with a hammer. Just to let you know. Control out.*

What the hell was going on tonight? Why all the freakyness? Were all the corner shops running a two-for-the-price-of-one special on Buckfast? Were the city's drug pushers giving out free samples of crystal meth again?

Unfortunately there was no reason. It would have been somehow reassuring if all this rabid behaviour had a defined cause – like in movies where the Earth passes through the tail of a comet and turns everyone into zombies. Despairingly, this was just Glasgow's feral youth doing what they do. Comet or no comet.

With my mind on such things I arrived at the last stop on my run only to find Mr Black-Pudding-Sucker sliding down his seat having fallen asleep and missed his stop.

'Wakey wakey!' I bellowed forth. As is usually the way I

had to bellow forth, fifth and sixth coz sleeping drunks never wake up on the first shout.

'Wha'? Where the hell are we, driver?'

'Knightswood. This is the last stop, I'm afraid this bus is finished for the night. I'm going back to the depot and you'll have to get off here.'

Now, usually I get hit with, 'Why did you not wake me up at my stop, ya bastard!?' Even if I were Marvo the Memory Man and could actually remember where all my hundreds of passengers were going every day, I still wouldn't get out my cab to wake their sorry arses up for the sake of my own safety. I've heard stories in the depot of sleepers going completely screwball when woken up.

'Oh! Sorry, man. I'm really drunk. I must have fallen asleep.'

That was a relief. Mr Black-Pudding-Sucker seemed to be of the mellow type so I offered to transfer him on to the next bus.

'Driver, I'm nearly home, just give us a lift along the street and I can just walk the rest of the way.'

'I'm not supposed to carry passengers when I'm not in service.'

'Pleeease! Just a wee bit along the road. I'll no do nothin' wrong! I'll behave!'

'Well, maybe just a few hundred yards, but only coz I'm going that way anyway.'

'Yes! Cheers, mucker!'

As we set off, he came shuffling down the bus and began to offer the kind of gratitude that you could really do without: 'Hey driver! You are the man! You are the best! You're one of the good guys!'

He then tried to open my cab door. 'Don't open that! I'm trying to drive the bus!'

'Shake hands, man! What can I do to repay you?' he asked.

'Erm, just give us a bite of your black pudding,' I said, jokingly.

'I'll show you my pudding!' he said and reached his right hand down the front of his jeans.

'Jesus Christ!' I blasphemed. 'Don't you dare! You better not be gonna pull out your goddamn –'

In retrospect, I think his cock would have been less lethal than what he did pull out from the front of his jeans: a twelve inch stainless steel blade on a black carbon fibre handle with integrated stud-lock. Death never looked so shiny.

Warrior Scotsman: Actually, now I think about it, I'm not sure which was more deadly – the cold steel in his right hand or the deep fried pig's blood in his left.

'Hey! That's some knife. Where did you get it?' I asked trying to keep him calm and wondering how the hell I got myself into this situation.

'I bought it from a shop in the toon. I only use it for self defence coz there's just so many mad bastards carrying knives these days.'

I wheezed and almost vomited with the irony of it.

'Aye, mad bastards,' I said. 'By the way, you do know that this bus has CCTV all over it, don't you?'

'Oh, shit! Let me off! Quick, open the door! Open the door!'

He thought that by getting away quickly he would be somehow too fast for the camera's to spot him and his knife. Last thing I saw was him staggering away down a side street stuffing the knife back down the front of his jeans. Hope he sliced off his genitalia. I vowed never again to give anyone a lift when not in service. Man, woman or child – you're getting kicked off at the terminus without a pang of guilt.

12

BOMB SCARE

Started my shift at the depot by getting one of the virginal new single deckers ready for a run to that in-growing toenail known as East Kilbride. Everything worked as it should, all systems were go and the interior was immaculately clean. The whole bus even smelled new. It was testimony to the skills of the night-time cleaning brigade. The most interesting member of this bunch of stalwarts was a stout, chain-smoking woman whom I called The Tuba. To me, she looked the way a tuba sounded. The Tuba never flinched at the prospect of having to clean up rivers of puke, puddles of piss and even shards of glass. 'Ye huv tae dig fur yer gold in this place,' she once said when I presented her with a particularly foul vehicle. Tuba, you are a gem.

However, as I rumbled along Great Western Road picking up chirping muppets and drunken kebab munchers, I thought it a shame that the bus would probably return to The Tuba looking more like a haggard old harlot than the chariot of chastity it was just now.

'Driver! (bang) (bang) (bang) Driver!'

'Whoa!' I said in reflex, having completely missed a silver-skinned muppet bumbling down the gangway of my bus.

'Driver! I've got something to tell you. I think you should know about this,' she whimpered.

BOMB SCARE

The Tuba and Her Magic Broom: Always up to her nuts in guts.

Okay, what had she done? I pulled the bus in to the side of the road fearing the worst. The very worst. Oh, Tuba! Get your Marigold's on! I opened my cab door and the little rumpler popped her head through. It seemed that I was averting my nostrils quite unnecessarily.

'Driver,' she whispered, 'there is unattended baggage that has been sitting on a chair for the whole way along the road. Well, in view of what happened on that bus in London, I think it's only right that I should tell you about it.'

Shit! (Metaphorically.)

We've been warned about this. If ever suspicious baggage turns up we are supposed to evacuate the bus and radio the control room, who would then send the police to investigate. Bearing in mind I was now in the city centre, I figured they may even close off some streets causing widespread disruption and panic.

Nevertheless, I thought it a good idea to at least take a look at the bag before I alerted control. Stepping out of the cab, I sensed the atmosphere on the bus was ripe with fear. All the pensioners were actually clinging to the seat in front of them as though readying themselves for action. I'm pretty sure if I suddenly shouted, 'Everyone down!' I could have had twenty muppets on their faces in a flash.

'Where's the bag, then?' I asked the lady.

'That's it there,' she said, and pointed a knobbly finger at a dark blue hold-all on the seat behind the driver's cab.

Holy Jesus! It was MY bag! I must have left it on the seat when I got the bus ready at the depot. Nutty bastard!

'Ah!' I said, not wanting to give myself away. 'Oh, don't worry about that. I'll just take it into my cab for safe keeping.'

'I think it's very unwise to touch it!' quivered the muppet.

'Don't worry, it's probably a home-made device. I know how to defuse these. Heh, heh!'

'Well, I think that's very unwise!' said the muppet as I lifted the bag into the cab. 'Very unwise indeed!'

Unwise? Let me tell you about unwise. Unwise is staying on a bus after the driver tells you he's going to defuse a bomb in his cab! Yes, they all just sat there muttering their discontent all the way to Argyle Street. Silly muppets.

On my last run of the night, I left East Kilbride and headed towards the city. Already I was thinking about my wee whisky and soul session when I got home. 'Freddie's Dead' by Curtis Mayfield and a nip of Glenmorangie should send me off nicely. Yes, I could almost taste it now.

But I came back down to Earth with a bump as I saw up ahead that all the traffic had stopped and there were flashing blue lights in the middle of the road. It seemed there had just been a very nasty car accident and the police had closed the road. Drat! They were turning all the traffic round and sending it back the way it came. The problem was I didn't know the surrounding area very well. How the hell was I going to get back on my route? It was all tight country roads round here and I was concerned about taking the bus down a dark road and bowling a cow.

I decided to honk my horn to attract the attention of a cop. Surely he could give me directions on where to go. So I hit the horn and opened the doors. I expected a big swarthy buffoon to muscle his way over and say 'Yeah? What da hell do you want?' and then point a large sausage-like finger in the best direction. But as usual, my expectations were ill-conceived.

In answer to my horn-honking, a diminutive little copper with extra shiny shoes came skipping over to my bus. 'Yeth?' he lisped.

'Um . . .' said I, like a rabbit caught in headlights. 'Do you know how I can get this bus back on its route? I need to get to the Cathkin roundabout without hitting any low bridges.'

'Ooh!' he bloomed like a posy of daffodils. 'I really don't know. I really juth don't know. All of your colleagueth have juth turned round and gone back the way they came.'

At that precise moment the car in front of me crossed into the oncoming lane, but instead of turning round and heading back, it just carried on! Straight into oncoming traffic moving at sixty miles per hour!

'Hey!' I shouted. 'That car has just gone the wrong way down the road!'

I anticipated the cop would yell some code words into his radio like 'Foxtrot Tango to control, we have a code 47 in progress, send Delta unit and a chopper.' But again, my expectations were a bit on the high side.

'Yeth, I thaw that,' said the cop sullenly and watched the car go. 'Woman driver, BITCH!' he spat with more spiteful resentment than if you had borrowed a drag queen's hairdryer without permission. Spooked, I made off down a country road in case I became the hapless victim of his feather boa at tonight's Cop Cabaret.

Catty Cop: This copper doesn't give tickets, he just goes in a huff and binges on chocolate cake.

Now completely lost, I stopped and opened the cab door to ask my only punter if he knew how to get to the Cathkin roundabout. But the little bastard had fallen asleep and was now dribbling down his jacket. No amount of shouting in his face could rouse the beast. Double drat!

So I just sort of drove around in the dark. It was scary not knowing where the road was going and I was nervously looking out for low bridges and tight bends. But, by some miracle, I found a round sign which gave me my bearings and managed to get the bus back on route in one piece.

Other poor drivers in similar situations have ripped the roof off deckers when forced off route. I doubt if even The Tuba's magic broom could do anything about fixing that.

13

HUMILIATION

I seem to be getting a lot of East Kilbride routes recently and am really bored with them. This evening I had yet another run to that stinking Greenhills terminus – our depot's favourite al fresco latrine. I wondered how people like Driver Ubu and Driver Stingball managed to hold down this job for decades without wanting to do themselves in. It was all beginning to feel like Groundhog Day to me. One week was just running into the next.

The traffic lights on Renfrew Street were at red so I took the opportunity to have a quick slug from my Lucozade bottle. As I did, a frail old lady hobbled down the bus. She tapped at my cab door like the pitter-patter of a little moth at your bedroom window.

'Driver, isn't it great that we've got all these bars now!'

I almost spat my Lucozade all over the inside of the windscreen. 'What? You like bars?' I asked, completely amazed.

'Oh yes! I don't know how I managed without them.'

'So, you like a drink, then? Which bar is your favourite?'

She gave me a strange look and then said: 'Well, probably this one here.'

'You've got to be kidding! That's Destiny! That's a nightclub! You don't go in there do you?'

'No! This bar here,' she said and tapped the handrail she was holding on to.

'Oh, bars! I thought you meant . . . oh, never mind.'

The lights turned green and I trundled round the corner to the bus stop. Before the little muppet stepped off the bus, she turned to me and said: 'This is a very shaky bus, driver. I think you should call your bus the vibrator bus.'

Think I'm gonna hurl! Screw the Lucozade – I need a double Jack Daniels.

Eventually I made it down to Argyle Street and picked up, amongst other pond life and bottom feeders, a drunken frog-like girl.

'How much is it?' said Froggy and plopped two pound coins into the coin slot.

'Hang on, where are you going?' I asked.

'I don't care!' she shouted and plopped another two pound coins into the slot.

'You want an all day ticket? Is that it?'

'I don't care!' she wailed again, and another two pound coins went plop.

'You want a weekly ticket?'

'I don't fucking care, right?'

Without waiting for any ticket to be printed she turned and waddled away up the bus. 'Prick!' she shouted, and sat down at the very back of the bus.

I had now been in the job long enough to be able to accurately *read* the bus. In time, all bus drivers develop a sixth sense of impending trouble; like a canary down a mine shaft sniffing for gas, or a gold fish that goes nuts before an earthquake. With Froggy Girl's continued outbursts, I could sense the bus was primed and ready for meltdown – a tinderbox waiting for a single spark.

Like a ned!

And I got one. The loathsome fiend boarded at Glasgow

Cross and was visibly disappointed that his desired seat at the back of the bus had been taken by the Froggy Girl.

'Pricks! You are all pricks!' came the Frog as the ned sat down on a vacant seat.

'It's you that's the fuckin' prick!' was the ned's reflex response.

The atmosphere on the bus ripened by the minute, and by Farm Cross in Rutherglen, my canary had fallen off its perch and my goldfish had flipped out of its bowl onto the floor.

'Hey, pricko!' shouted the Frog at the ned.

The Ned turned and shot her a look that reminded me of a red dot from the laser sights on a rifle. The kind of look that says: *You feelin lucky, punk? Well, do ya?*

'What you lookin' at ya prick?!' bellowed Froggy.

With that the ned's limited self-control expired and he pulled the trigger. Jumping to his feet, he bolted up to the back of the bus to give the Frog a good thrashing. My hand went to the emergency radio button to get help, but something made me pause. Despite the fact that neds are vermin, especially ones who think nothing of bashing up a female on a bus, I was overcome with a feeling of Nature taking its course.

No, I don't mean I sat there and wet myself. What I mean is that I now thought of every shift as going 'on safari'. I drove through dangerous territory looking out for wild animals. Some want to fight you, others want to fuck you. Thus it has been for the last three billion years since life began.

Just like David Attenborough doesn't interfere when a lion is tearing the throat out of a gazelle, why should I interfere when a ned wants to beat a froggy girl to a pulp?

It's Nature's way. The strong survive and the weak must die. The State may provide artificial refuge for those on the fringes of society but on *my* vehicle it is Natural Selection that reigned. That's right, you've got Charles Darwin driving your bus. Let the bloodbath begin!

Or so it would have been if an old man with a walking stick hadn't jumped up and wrestled the ned away. Ned and muppet were locked in a sumo-like embrace for a full two minutes as the ned tried to get past, but the man muppet held firm. The Frog was but a hip replacement away from A&E.

Puny Ned boy loses scrummage to elderly Man Muppet while Froggy the Frogster bellows on.

The ned wasn't finished though. He darted down the bus shouting 'Driver, open the door!' So I did, and the ned bolted off the bus. I saw him in my mirror run round to the back of the bus and pull the emergency door open so he could get at the Frog. Cunning! There were screams from the rear of the bus as the ned tried to climb up for a suitable punching angle.

It was then I decided that I couldn't be bothered with

the paperwork of an assault on my bus so I just accelerated away hoping the ned would fall back out the emergency door. And he did. Cool! He gave chase but I took a liberty with a red light and was clear.

Well, so much for 'Wonder Driver' and my desire to provide a good service to passengers. How distant those innocent memories become. This evening I had found the prospect of a ned thumping a loud-mouthed frogster to be quite attractive. I had even found the shambling efforts of a man muppet to stop the fight to be quite entertaining too. What was I turning into? And what about running that red light? My journey to the dark side was well underway.

Ten minutes later, completely unfazed by her near-pummelling, Froggy Girl came down the bus to get off at her stop. 'Driver, I think you've got a very sexy body, what time do you finish?' (You see? Fight or Fuck! It has always been the way!)

'Erm, too late for you I think.'

'Can I just do anything I want to you? Would you let me? Would you just let me humiliate you?'

Is it just me or is there something off-putting about a girl like that? I decided to punish her.

'You like humiliation do you?' I asked.

'Aye! I'm into all that.'

'Right, I'll go first. What's the capital city of Belgium?'

'Wha'?'

'Great! Now, what's seven times nine?'

'Um, swenty-seven or something. Forty-six? Why? What you talkin' about?'

'You feeling humiliated yet?'

'You're a bastard!' she said and left the bus.

She's right, you know. Humiliation really did feel good!

14
THE ARSEHOLE DISPOSAL UNIT

Double decker buses are seen as nothing more than play ground rides by drunken, rowdy passengers. So much so that only single deckers are put on the more notorious runs in an act of damage limitation like the gut wrenching, barbed wire sandwich that goes to Paisley.

However, my heart sank when I saw the old, crappy, smoke-belching double decker arrive for me at the relief point. Bastard! Putting a decker on the fearsome Paisley run was a bit like putting a bouncy castle into a psychiatric ward. *Weeeeeeeeee! It's playtime!*

This was all Jelly Baby's doing. He was responsible for assigning buses to routes and must have been feeling extra vindictive today to stick an ancient Dennis Dominator on the tortuous Paisley run. In the Partick bothy earlier, Driver Fuzclaw was saying that Jelly Baby recently had a run in with the The Manager about driver shortages and crappy buses and not being able to maintain service levels on all routes. 'We just don't have the drivers to cover all the shifts!' I often heard him complain in the depot. 'And even if we did have the drivers, we wouldn't have enough buses to put them in.' I doubt The Manager would have offered a sympathetic ear. Maybe Jelly Baby was just taking it all out on us by putting old scrappers on notoriously busy runs.

Anyway, three wee neds got on my bus at Central Station

and did their best to hide their bottles of Buckfast as they boarded. The youngest was only about thirteen but was quite the Snoop Dog with his earrings, gold chains and sovereign rings. 'Take it easy, driver,' said the little artful dodger.

Of course, they went straight upstairs and sat at the very back. 'Yes! It's got no CCTV!' I heard one of them shout. All the way down Paisley Road West they stamped their feet, shrieked mercilessly, sang sectarian songs and kicked their Buckfast bottles around the floor. The passengers on the lower deck were mumbling stuff like 'That's ridiculous!' and 'That shouldn't happen!' and the obligatory 'Fuck's sake!' while all the time praying that the ceiling did not cave in above them.

A worried little muppet came down the bus to get off at Cardonald.

'Hey, driver!' said the muppet. 'Can you not hear that? Can you not hear what's going on up there? For Christ's sake!'

'Yep,' said I.

'Well, what the hell are you gonna do about it?'

'What do you mean?'

'Get them sorted out!'

'You want me to get out my cab, go upstairs and give them a stern talking to?'

'Yes!'

'Don't think so. I signed up to drive a bus and give tickets. If the company gave me a stab vest and a tazer gun, then I might consider crowd control. Until then I stay in my cab.'

'That's it! I'm taking your number! I'm putting in a complaint about you!'

THE ARSEHOLE DISPOSAL UNIT

And there you have the final proof:

$$\text{Drunken Delinquents} + \text{Moany Muppet} = \text{Complaint Against Driver}$$

Calling the cops to get rid of the delinquents wouldn't have helped anyway. It would have just transferred the trouble on to another bus, freaked out another driver, frightened other passengers and caused more damage.

It's times like these that I would like to flick a switch in the driver's cab and turn the upstairs back seat into a big death grinder. A sort of big combine-harvester-come-steam-roller jobby. I would dearly like to see the pricks' faces as they drowned in a high-speed whirlpool of blades:

Dear Volvo, Could you please install an Arsehole Disposal Unit to the rear seat of all your new buses. Thank you.

After the shredding, cutting, mashing and mangling of the arseholes, the rollers, blades, fly wheels and gears of the Arsehole Disposal Unit would wind down and the seat would return to its original appearance. Less three wee neds of course.

Surely that was better than the reality of getting to the Paisley terminus and finding that the drunken arseholes had left an ankle deep puddle of piss upstairs and had used a blade to cut away the rubber from the windows? Yes, a window was flapping out of it's frame and could have quite easily fallen out on top of a pedestrian, killing them without so much as a 'how d'you do'.

Just like my first broken window at Cathkin, the Control Room just sent me back to the depot to get a replacement bus. In a way, the neds had done everyone a favour by getting this stinking bucket of bolts off the road. The Tuba did not bat an eyelid when she came aboard with her magic broom. I had come to the conclusion that she smoked constantly to mask the awful smell of beer and urine that clung to buses. Very wise. As she got busy, I stepped off the bus and met Driver Ubu in the yard.

'Where did that happen? Up the Drum?' he asked, pointing at my upstairs window which was still hanging out.

'Paisley,' I said.

'Suppose it gets you off your shift for half an hour. Lucky bugger.'

Lucky bugger? Despite everything that I'd seen so far, it still came as a shock to learn that some drivers actually looked forward to getting their windows broken just so they could get a few minutes away from the public. I wasn't there quite yet, but I had to admit feeling quite relieved at getting away from that decrepit Dominator and those neds. But surely my idea of an Arsehole Disposal Unit built into the back seat of every decker was a cleaner, quicker and more elegant method of getting away from neds than hoping they smash your windows?

15

BOWLING FOR COMPO

Would you believe it – I was actually developing a taste for the greasy stodge served up by Chowder Chops in his slop shop canteen. I had even come in early to fill up on his dish of the day before I take to the wheel. Today, it was beef brisket with chips and baked beans in gigantic portions. My bus driver's belly was developing nicely.

As I munched, I noticed that Driver Gollum was still giving me funny looks after I tailed him last month. But then, I was still giving Stingball funny looks for shafting me the month before. No doubt Stingball, in turn, was eying some other driver for pumping him. And so on throughout the whole depot. Wasn't there supposed to be some kind of brotherhood amongst drivers out there on the road? If there was, I was yet to see it.

'Ye were right tae thtay in yer cab,' said Driver Chucklemumble. I had just told him about the muppet last week who threatened to write a complaint if I didn't go upstairs and sort out those Buckfast-swilling neds. 'I've been doin' thith joab over twenty yearth and I don't get oot ma cab for nae body!'

'Yes, I just stayed put. Those neds were really rowdy. No CCTV either,' I said.

'It'th no like the nedth were gonna say, "Oh, thorry driver, we'll calm doon noo and thtop drinkin' oor Buckie. Thankth for bringin' oor anti-thothial behaviour to oor attenthion.

We've learned oor lethon today and no mithtake!" No, you'd get a boattle right in the kither! Theh! Theh!'

'Don't listen tae him!' shouted Driver Gollum. 'Anyone starts any shit on my bus and I'm oot the cab and up the stairs tae sort it oot! The punters are all scared o' me!'

'Aye, but you're always gettin' intae trouble for that!' countered Chucklemumble.

'I don't care, anyone starts anythin' on my bus, I'm always the one tae finish it. End of story.'

'You're aff yer heid!' said Chucklemumble.

Either way, the predicament of the driver was unenviable; stay in your cab and risk a complaint, or get out your cab and risk a bottle in the face. I left Gollum and Chucklemumble arguing the toss as I went out to the relief point to pick up my bus. Hopefully, this evening's shift would not bring any nasty surprises. But hope didn't count for much in this job.

The first part of my shift was all a-shriek with what seemed like every shrieker in Glasgow coming on my bus at the same time – shrieking: countless shrieking school kids, three shrieking babies, two shrieking she-neds and one shrieking fat man. Well, the fat guy didn't actually shriek but his appalling stench did plenty of shrieking on his behalf.

I'm not kidding, this guy's brutal funk was almost a physical assault. It was like a tangible echo of the carnage generated by all wars past and a tip of the hat to all that was evil in the world today. He was the true champion of all things that slither and moulder and ... hang on a minute ... INCOMING! ...

... BANG! went a stone off my cab window as I approached the Summerston terminus. Without thinking, my arms were off the steering wheel and flapping all about the cab in the kind of reflex defensive actions that make you feel like a right tit afterwards.

But credit where credit is due, it really was a well-aimed shot! A perfectly executed cab window strike from over fifty yards. Obviously thrown by the practiced hand of a true professional, it deserved so much more. A crack in the glass at least.

With nerves now ruffled, I did not enjoy sitting at the Summerston terminus for ten long minutes. I jumped with every distant scream and dog bark, thinking the stone-throwing neds were coming back to finish what they started. All around me, glistening on the road, were millions of little ice-cubes of shattered bus window that had been obliterated on previous nights of ultra-violence. Fortunately, this was a week night and the local Young Team had opted merely to nibble rather than bite.

I was starting to come round to Driver Ubu's way of thinking and wished they had actually cracked the glass. 'It gets you off your shift for half an hour', he had said. Yes, I'd far rather be back at the depot getting a replacement bus than sitting out here wondering what else might come out of the night at me.

But, still in one piece, I left the terminus and literally tip-toed through the dark streets (not easy in a decker), all the time checking nearby alleyways for movement and wondering what lay in wait at the bus stops up ahead. At Summerston ASDA I picked up a double dose of social blight in the form of a pimp and his hooker. Mr Pimp was dressed smartly in a leather jacket (*Gianni Versace* was the label, I believe), dark blue Chinos, polished shoes and, naturally, a bling-bling pinky-ring.

But in horrifying contrast, his wire-framed hooker was an abstract piece of modern art sculpture – *Cadaver In Denim*.

Her spaced-out eyes, slack jaw and protruding tongue made for a wonderful smack-induced facial prolapse. As for her stylistic leanings, compared to Mr Pimp, her designer label was *Papier Mache*.

They both flashed a pass at me and, of course, went straight upstairs. However, all the way down Maryhill Road, while Mr Pimp mumbled into his cell phone, the Hooker tottered up and down the top deck without holding on to any handrails. Very unwise, considering her natural unsteadiness. It was almost as though she wanted to be thrown about, wanted to be injured. Maybe the thought of going into town tonight and giving hand relief to countless double-Y chromo neanderthals in freezing alleyways seemed so unpalatable, even for this googly-eyed harlot, that an easier revenue stream was preferable. Like a sure-fire, watertight, cannot-fail compensation claim against the bus company.

At Renfield Street in the city centre I was doing a steady 10mph in slow moving traffic; not accelerating, not braking and not turning. I watched the CCTV monitor with despair as the Hooker shambled over to the top of the stairs and cried, 'Whaaa!' and launched herself down the stairwell. What a noise she made as she hit every stair on the way down . . .

'(WUMP) OOF! (WUMP) OUCH! (WUMP) AARG! (WUMP) BWOAGH! (WUMP) HOEY! (WUMP) GRUMPH!'

At the bottom of the stairs she unfolded herself and began shrieking: 'Ya' bastard! Ya' prick! That was your fault ya' fuckin' maniac! Did everyone see that? Did everyone see him make me fa' doon them stairs? There's a bus full o' witnesses! You're gettin' sued, ya' bastard!'

THE BLOODBUS

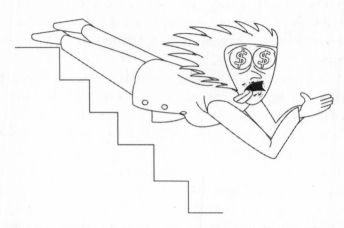

Tumble Junkie: How to fund one's next smack hit. The choice was simple - throw yourself down a bus stair well and put in a claim, or go out and get rear-ended by a sailor. I think she chose wisely.

I pulled the bus into the side of the road as Pimp 'n' Hooker shuffled up to my cab door.

'Right!' she screamed. 'I want your name, I want your address and I want your number. Right noo!'

'Nope,' I said calmly.

'I've got bruises all over ma fuckin' heid! Give's the pen in yer shirt pocket so I can write doon all your details.'

'Nope.'

'You were driving like a maniac! Everyone oan the bus saw me fa'! Give's your pen!'

'Nope.'

At this point a normal passenger came down the bus, a middle-aged woman who had boarded at the previous stop. 'Driver, she's got a right to know your number.'

'Do you realise I could end up getting sacked over this? Sacked for nothing,' I said.

'Look, I'm tired and I just want to get home,' said the woman. 'Here,' she said to the Hooker, 'I don't have a pen but you can use my eye liner pencil to at least take the bus number.'

The Hooker grinned like a plotting pit-bull and actually tried to embrace her, but the woman grimaced and wrestled herself away.

'I really don't care, I'm not taking sides,' said the woman. 'I just want to get home.'

The Hooker and Mr Pimp were now standing on the pavement writing down the bus number. Actually, it was Mr Pimp who was scribbling the number on the back of the Hooker's right hand (I got the feeling that he was more at home with the whole reading/writing thing).

'Will you be ma witness?' shouted the Hooker to the normal woman who was still standing on the bus.

'Um, well, I don't think the driver was doing anything wrong. I would say you just lost your own footing and fell.'

The Hooker scowled at her like a Dobermann.

With Pimp 'n' Hooker off the bus, I realised this was my chance to escape. I closed the doors, released the break and hit the gas. But just as I did, the Hooker gave a mighty screech and thrust her right hand in between the closing doors. Ouch! Normally I would have stopped and made sure the person was uninjured, but not tonight. No, sir! Tonight I sped up, and if I took her severed hand with me then so be it!

Hopefully the wretch didn't have the full bus number on her hand when I fled. Even if she did, hopefully it'd be smudged beyond recognition after she jammed her hand in the door. Ooh! That still gave me goosebumps!

In retrospect, I might have actually done her a good turn

by crushing her boney little mitt. After all, for a woman in her profession, having a 'honey-pot' hand can only be an advantage – enables a more natural grip of her client. Yes, that's right, get back to work down that alley and give those double-Y chromos a hand-job to remember, coz you ain't gettin' no compo tonight!

If this had happened to me a few weeks ago, I think I would have just abandoned the bus in shock and gone home. But, having seen how miserable and pathetic some members of the great unwashed can be, tonight's incident aroused only my contempt. The Company may have taught me how to drive a bus, but it's experiences such as this that made me a bus driver. And I think I was finally there.

16
TERMINATORS

There had very nearly been a fist fight in the Partick bothy between Driver Ubu and Driver Humpty. Some bright spark had brought in a set of dominoes to relieve the boredom and all hell had broken loose. An argument about whether they were playing 'block' rules or 'draw' rules had escalated into a screaming match. Although the stakes were little more than spare copper coins, neither driver wanted to lose face in front of their peers, so the dominoes ended up all over the floor. I wondered if a funeral party had been gathering next door like when drunken Gollum stormed in and kicked off. Space for any more in that coffin?

However, their inflated egos were punctured by news from the King of gossip himself, Driver Fuzz Claw, that Stingball had been rushed off his bus and into hospital after complaining of chest pains. Strangely, it seemed to come as no surprise to anyone in the bothy. It had happened several times before and, everyone agreed, he was due again about now. Driver Stingball was always an avid fan of the depot slop shop as his rotund physique showed. He was also a heavy smoker. In fact every time I picked up a bus from him, my right hand would always end up stinking of nicotine just from touching the steering wheel. But, even though he was a renowned bastard for tailing other drivers, we all wished him a speedy recovery.

After this sombre but short pause, Ubu and Humpty carried on where they had left off just before Fuzz Claw had delivered the news – at each other's throats. I was actually relieved when my break finished and I had to leave the shouting and yelling to pick up my bus at the relief point. It was the evening rush hour and the bus was heaving. As I trundled down to East Kilbride (again), I just looked forward to getting through the bus station and up to the sanctuary of the terminus.

Ah, the terminus. A shining beacon of light that beckoned you to the end of your route. A passenger-free oasis where the weary driver can catch his breath, read his paper, stretch his legs, have a snack and piddle up against his back tyre. Terminus time is driver's time. Terminus time is sacred. A far cry from the Partick bothy.

But don't be fooled. Terminus time is not always such a carnival of debauchery. Many termini are located in the deepest, darkest recesses of the most godforsaken ghettos in Western Europe. Real bandit country.

'Right! That's it! I'm going home to get my dad and my two swords!' I once heard a ned shout to his foes during a running gang fight at a particularly nasty terminus. En guard! Also, the seemingly well organised legions of Curtain Twitchers can prove equally as deadly. At Robroyston, for example, I threw an apple core out my cab window, but before it even hit the ground, a local grumpy man who was secretly keeping watch came huffing and puffing out of his house wearing only his pyjamas and slippers. Standing a little distance away, he took snap after snap of me with his camera phone. All for an apple core!

Had he come a little closer, I would have pointed out that his street was already covered by a three-foot-thick layer of garbage, bus glass and dog shit, and that there was a discarded sofa and burnt out car just round the corner. A little perspective here, please? After all, if a truck runs over your head, you don't go around complaining about the pimple on your arse.

However, even roaming death-neds and pyjama'd curtain twitchers don't compare to the biggest threat to a happy terminus: The Terminators. These are people who stay on the bus all the way to the terminus, and once there, they still don't get off.

Terminators come in all shapes and sizes, but always seem to have one thing in common – they always magically materialize when you are dying for a pee. On several occasions I have arrived at a terminus, jumped out my cab thinking the bus was empty and started undoing my flies only to hear those despairing words from somewhere up the back: 'Driver, where the hell are we?' Beware the Terminators. Bus drivers' burden.

I picked up Three Little Pigs at East Kilbride bus station. The oldest piglet was no more than twelve years old and sported the most astounding face of freckles.

'Does this bus go to the Lindsayfield terminus?' he asked.

'What? Erm, uh-huh, yep,' was my distracted reply. My God, his freckles were almost three dimensional! It was as though he had wet his face and dunked it straight into a bowl of dry cornflakes. A not-so-healthy way to start the day.

Anyway, Freckles and his two snotsters paid their fare and clumped up to the top deck. As we set off, I checked my CCTV screen to see the tumbling little romp-sprites throwing each other over seats, clunking each other with an empty can of Tennent's lager and throwing copies of the Metro out of windows.

'Sit doon an' shut up!' shouted a peeved old man. But 'sit doon an' shut up' they did not, and so on it went.

As I approached the terminus, I had a growing sense of unease. Firstly, because I was now dying for a pee, and secondly, because the Three Little Pigs hadn't come down to get off yet. Now with the whole bus to themselves, they whooped and yelled and freaked and shrieked. To my ears it was an argument for corporal punishment . . . on buses . . . by drivers.

As my mind dreamed up new uses for electric cattle prods, my bladder desired only my back tyre. I needed the terminus. Badly. Where did the little giblets say they were going? Oh, yes, Lindsayfield. Wait a minute: this bus doesn't go to Lindsayfield! It goes to the Gardenhall terminus which is over a mile away from Lindsayfield!

Shit! I screwed up! I told them I went to Lindsayfield! Now I'm going to have three little punk-ass Terminators spoiling my down-time. Worse than that, with Terminators on the bus, there was no way I was going to have the privacy to relieve myself, and boy did I need to do that right now. I would have gladly sold my soul to Satan for a porcelain urinal, my right arm for a rusty bucket or even my left testicle for that empty beer can rattling around upstairs. Yes, the Devil does drive a hard bargain.

Having now reached the Gardenhall terminus I switched the engine off and got out my cab.

'That's the end of the line!' I shouted up the stairs.

There was a sudden thud of silence from the clowners. Freckles was first to come down, followed eventually by his two grimy drones.

Freckles piped up: 'We're going to Lindsayfield.'

'Well, this bus doesn't go to Lindsayfield.'

'But at the bus station you said that you went to Lindsayfield!'

'Did I?'

'Yeah!' they answered in unison.

'Well, I'm afraid I don't. I made a mistake, you'll have to get off here and get another bus.'

My plan was to get them off the bus just long enough to go upstairs and have my wicked way with that empty beer can I had just bought for a testicle. But as they sulked their way off the bus I could see their bottom lips start to tremble. It suddenly assailed me that these hopeless little fiends were totally lost and completely shitting themselves. From clowners to downers in ten seconds. Oh, well, it's a learning experience for them, I thought. As the Irish say, it'll 'tighten' them.

With the Three Little Pigs now standing on the pavement I closed the doors, switched off all the lights and bolted upstairs in the dark. Having located the empty beer can after some tentative groping, I quickly un-crushed it ready for filling. I knelt so that passengers on passing deckers would not get a shock and then dropped my trousers. The moment was nigh.

However, when my old fella knows that relief is imminent he can get a bit over zealous. Just as I was trying to line up with the frustratingly small hole in the beer can, I could hold back the tide no longer. Sploosh! A jet of urine ricocheted off the top of the can and drenched the front of my shirt. Dribbles of pee sprayed out all over the floor of the bus and down into the crotch of my trousers. I was caught in a stinking tsunami and sinking fast.

I had to properly line up my nudger with the hole, but in the thick darkness that meant actual physical contact

Fountain of Filth: The quest for the Dark Hole is a treacherous one.

between me and the can. Putting aside all fears of the wraith who might have been drinking out of the can with his chapped and ulcerated lips, I thrust forth and made contact with the cold aluminium. With a tingle up my spine I found the hole and filled the sucker to the brim.

I shudder to think how many casual relations I've had with empty beer cans and Buckfast bottles on the top deck of my bus. Especially when you consider the oral health of the rogues who leave them behind. It's like playing Russian roulette with your member every time – you just need to be unlucky once. So far I've always come up smelling of roses, but like anything else in life, all it takes is one pair of raw, festering lips and you're pissing fire for a month.

Out on the pavement, down below, I heard Freckles talking into his phone. His voice was all a-quiver and a-mumble but I could make out something about 'the bus' and 'the driver' and 'mistake'. I figured he was calling his mother who would now be jumping up and down *spitting* freckles with the thought of her darling little pug being left to the tender mercies of some scurrilous bus driver. Moi?

There was no doubt in my mind she was going to race down to the terminus in her car with a meat skewer and bread knife and carve herself a turkey. So, quicker than thinking, I cleaned up most of the piss with a few scraps of Metro and threw the can out the window. Although it landed with a wonderful 'gloink!', I felt dirty and ashamed. I will never again complain about any passenger who comes on my bus stinking of piss. There will be a nod of understanding between us.

'Listen!' I said to the little punks after coming back down stairs, 'I've got fifteen minutes before I'm due to leave here. Just take a seat and I'll quickly drive you over to Lindsayfield and we'll call it quits. Okay?' Maternal wrath is a powerful motivator.

The three slunk aboard and did not make a sound until they slunk off again at Lindsayfield.

'Thank you, driver,' they said. But my mind was preoccupied with other thoughts. Such as 'Should I rub a blob of Blistex into the end of my lingam?'

If you are female and your boyfriend or spouse is a bus driver, a great present for Christmas would be a little plastic funnel so your lover doesn't have to risk touching his manhood against tainted beer cans. It really is in your interests to do this. Otherwise you may wonder why you're feeling unusually itchy.

17

BRAIN DAMAGE

Started my shift by picking up the Paisley bus from Driver Guy Smiley. 'So, she just threw herself doon yer stairs?' he asked.

'Aye,' I said, 'she got on at Summerston ASDA with her pimp, then on Renfield Street she just took a nosedive down the stairs and went nuts about suing for compo.'

'Was she a junkie?'

'Yup.'

'Those bastards will dae absolutely anythin' to get money,' he said. 'See Driver Stingball who's in hospital the noo with a bad ticker? Well, some junkie nutcase threw himself in front of his bus just so he would be able to put in a claim. Left Stingball traumatized, so it did.'

'Did the company pay out?'

'Course they paid oot! It's cheaper tae admit liability and blame the driver than it is tae fight it through the courts. It's easy money for the junkie scum. Always make sure you get lots of witnesses or else they'll just try and pin it on you.'

'Shit! That's one thing I didn't get. I was just too concerned with getting the hell away.'

'You just better hope the CCTV will back you up if you get pulled in tae the office. That reminds me, I've got my own troubles tae think aboot.' As Guy Smiley left the cab he informed me that he'd just been called to attend court as a witness to a particularly vicious stabbing on his bus.

'Did you actually see it happen?' I asked while typing my details into the ticket machine.

'Nope. But I knew for sure the guy had been stabbed,' he said, completely unfazed.

'How did you know?'

'He was runnin' aboot the bus with a big hole in his belly.'

Ask a silly question.

'But the weird thing is,' continued Guy Smiley, 'there was nae blood. Not a drop! Mind you, that piss-taking Manager in the depot is no givin' me paid leave tae go to court. He's making me use one of my holiday days instead! Prick!'

Nice to see Guy Smiley had got his priorities right.

As well as junkies, I was really beginning to see just how much of a problem knives were in Glasgow. I thought back to the black pudding muncher who had pulled a knife when I gave him a 'Not In Service' lift. By his appearance, I would never have thought he had a knife down his jeans. Although shocked at the time, I don't actually think he would have used it on me. But, Driver Guy Smiley made me realize just how lucky I had been.

After setting off, I became aware that the bus was an absolute howler. Everything shook, whined, squeaked, rattled, hissed, groaned, screeched and clattered – a real cantankerous old lady of the depot. Rain dribbled down the *inside* of the windscreen and the rubber seal designed to secure the side windows of the cab had gone, leaving them rattling in their frame. This ol' bucket was really beginning to shake my teeth loose. It got so bad that I had to drive along with my fingers in my ears and steer with my elbows. I suspect Jelly Baby must have had another blow out with The Manager.

Mind you, it had become apparent that most drivers

disliked being on the Paisley run at the best of times, so it really wouldn't have mattered what bus I got. Alright, that's an understatement, most drivers *hated* the Paisley run with the kind of passion most of us reserved for only our worst haemorrhoids. The clientele who frequent this razor run remind me of the cast of Michael Jackson's 'Thriller' video, all desperately clawing at your door whilst gnawing on kebab flesh. Prayers of absolution will not help any driver who forgets his wooden stake, crucifix and holy water.

Near the back of the bus, a nedette was screaming into her phone, 'Gary! Why are you being like this? You're just saying that coz you're drunk! (pause) Oh my God! Don't you dare say I've got an attitude! I've no got a fuckin' attitude, right? (pause) Oh my God! How can you say that? It's you that's got the fuckin' attitude!'

That's right, if someone accuses you of having an 'attitude', the best way of proving your innocence is to verbally beat them to a pulp with an even bigger and more malignant helping of 'attitude' – I'll show you just how much fuckin' attitude I don't fuckin' have!

At Finnieston, I picked up an elderly muppet of the short-squat variety – a real 'baller'. She humped a wheelie-bag of oddments up the stairs with a twitter and a mutter and a bibbety bobbety boo. Unfortunately she added to my headache by clattering her walking stick against everything within cat-swinging distance. Just because some muppets have a bad hip shouldn't mean that bus drivers have to risk losing an eye.

After I printed her ticket, she made for the seat directly behind my cab and plumped herself down, knocking her walking stick against the back of my cab as she went. There was another muppet in the adjacent seat, and when one muppet chances upon another, there is a bloom of recognition as they mutually identify a member of their own species – they recognise 'self'. You see the same reaction when a mirror is placed in front of an orangutan.

Before I had time to release the handbrake, both muppets had bonded and were doing the muppet equivalent of picking ticks and lice out of each other's fur.

'That's such a high step. How are pensioners supposed to get on and off the bus. It's ridiculous!'

'Yes, it's ridiculous!'

(Knock went the walking stick.)

'I used to get a different bus up on Great Western Road but they changed the route and now I've got to get this one instead.'

'Aye, they keep changing it, it's scandalous!'

'Scandalous!'

(Knock)

'I feel sorry for people who can't see very well, standing at a bus stop waiting for a bus that's not going to show.'

Yes, I think there was a perverse logic to that.

We set off and the noise from my clattering cab drowned out their conversation. However, I could still feel each thud from her 'knocking-stick' on the back of my cab as she fidgeted. It reminded me of what it must have been like for drivers of old horse drawn hansom cabs when the toffs used to bang their cane on the ceiling and shout, 'I say, driver, I'll give you an extra farthing if you can make that beast go any faster!'

Bus drivers don't get farthings. Or toffs for that matter. At best, you might be given half a bag of lemon drops when the bingo comes out. Bless.

As I pulled away from a bus stop at Blythswood Square

there was another knock, followed this time by an altogether more sinister thud. I felt this thud through my feet, but I felt the ensuing 'Waaaaaahhh!' through my very soul. A collective gasp from the rest of the bus sucked a black hole in the space-time continuum before anyone spoke again.

'Oh my God! Get it off her! Get it off her!' shouted a man.

I pulled in to the side of the road, popped my head out the cab door and was witness to a scene of panic and confusion. Two men were lifting a large, rectangular board off the little 'knocker' muppet whose arms were now uselessly flapping under it.

'Driver, that board fell doon aff the wa' on to that poor wumin's heid!' said one of the men.

Muppet Clunk: Keep on hitting a bus and, eventually, the bus will hit back.

I stepped out my cab to have a quick look and discovered the sad truth. There was a large and extremely heavy inspection panel behind the driver's cab which gave the engineers access to a fuse box. Usually this panel was held in place by four screws and two brackets, but on this rickety old boneshaker, it was held up by ONE screw (which had lost its thread anyway) and NO brackets. Knocker muppet must have loosened it with her incessant knockings, so all it needed was for me to accelerate away from a bus stop and WHAM! – instant tenderized muppet.

'I'm alright!' proclaimed the muppet as she passed through various stages of suffering in front of me.

'Are you sure?' I asked. 'I should maybe get an ambulance just to be on the safe side.'

'No! I'm alright!' she said, and stood up to brush away the dust that had come off the inspection panel.

My God, she seemed absolutely fine! Thank goodness little baller muppets are so well insulated by numb, fleshy, boneless layers of redundant anatomy. With the physique of a marshmallow, this resilient little flubber-muppet must have used her stout overabundance to absorb the full force of impact. Her insatiable appetite for cakes, scones and biscuits had just saved her life.

'Well, okay, but I'll need to take your details anyway for my report,' I said. I didn't actually intend handing the report in to the depot lest they tried to somehow pin it on me. I just wanted to deter the muppet from writing her own complaint, in which case they would definitely try to pin it on me.

She approached my cab and began whispering her name and address through the door. However, five drunken bastards had spotted me at the side of the road and decided they wanted on.

(BANG) (BANG) (BANG) 'Gonnae open the door?'

I opened the door.

The drunks paused, thinking the muppet was getting off. But after a second or two their patience ran out. 'Christ! Are you gettin' aff or what, missus?'

The muppet did not reply, I think she was still a bit dazed. I replied on her behalf, 'There's been a wee incident on the bus and I'm taking this passenger's details.'

'I don't fuckin' care! I'm getting rained on oot here!' He barged on to the bus, past the muppet and stomped away up the back. I didn't get a fare from two of his friends either, but on the bloodcurdling Paisley run, getting two fares out of five is not bad.

After contacting the Control Room to let them know about the incident, I was hopeful they would send me back to the depot to get a better bus. Wrong. They just sent round a wee man with a screwdriver to fix the inspection panel back up again with the correct screws and brackets.

'Anyone injured?' asked the wee man.

'Well, no one needed an ambulance, but . . .'

'Right, continue in service, driver.'

Doh! There's really no winning when you get on a bus in Glasgow – if the passengers don't kill you, the bus will.

18

THE ELECTRIC SCARECROW

A cold January sun drained the colour from Drumchapel's bunkered avenues and gloomy alleyways. The first snow of winter gave the grubby township a deceptively sterile aura by covering most of the garbage and urban tumbleweed, which on windy days is carried aloft and I'm sure must show up on weather radar.

But today I was feeling quite relieved. I had heard nothing about last week's muppet clunk, or the junkie who threw herself down the stairs a couple of weeks before that. All of her, 'You're getting sued, ya bastard!' must have just been hot air. Hopefully the CCTV hard drive would have been wiped by now anyway, so no one could prove a thing.

Saw Driver Gollum going in the opposite direction and he gave me a wave. Hopefully our little awkward patch was at an end. He was definitely not someone you wanted to get on the wrong side of. Especially now he was going though a bad patch with his girlfriend and had recently been in trouble for going up to her house and kicking the door in. I made sure I waved back.

As I drove up to the terminus, I took a left-hand turn into a narrow road and was surprised at what was blocking my way – another little scraggy junkie woman. This one was arse-down on the snowy pavement with her legs dangling out into the middle of the road. That's gotta be cold! Maybe last night's punters had been a little too rough with her and now she had to cool herself in the snow. But I couldn't concern myself with what fires may have been raging in her loin, I had to get my bus to the terminus. So I slowed to a crawl hoping she would retract her legs and I could pass. But, evidently her brain had flown south for the winter on wings of impure smack and left her body behind, because she just sat there, stiller than a frozen statue.

I was forced to stop and honk my horn. Her head turned towards me with all the frustrating slowness of a giant satellite dish tracking across the sky. Behind matted hair, her eyes gazed out from the back of two sunken ruts and focused on my vehicle. Recognising that it was *just a bus,* her malicious, tight-lipped grin resembled a flatulent tear in a pair of grubby breeches. She wasn't going to do me any favours at all.

So, with all due caution, I mounted the kerb and steered round her. Whatever nebula she was tripping through, she seemed quite content to stay there. I should maybe discharge my civic responsibility and tell Central Control about this, I thought.

However, having reached the terminus, instead of calling Control, I became somewhat preoccupied by the performance of a three-legged dog lolloping around near the skeleton of a burnt-out car. He was going completely nuts in the snow and was an absolute joy to watch. Then a woman appeared at the door of the bus and broke my reverie. 'One into the toon, driver,' she croaked.

'By the way, I'm not due to leave for another twenty minutes,' I said. 'If you walk up the hill to that bus stop you'd get a bus into town a lot quicker.'

'I know, but I'm too hungover to walk up the hill, I'll just stay on this bus, if that's okay?'

'Fair enough, take a seat.'

She sat down and I looked out the window again. The three-legged dog had been joined at the car wreck by two other skinny mongrels. They were all sitting down now, no doubt engaged in divvying up the junkie on the road amongst themselves. Nothing goes to waste here.

But it was not to be for the canine scavengers. Two cops drove past, spotted the junkie, stopped, reversed back and brazenly poached the dog's dinner from under their noses. With the force currently being throttled by a funding crisis, there will be prime cuts of marinated doper on the police station dinner table tonight. What a find! Final score: Pigs 1 – Dogs 0.

I set off into town and got as far as St George's Cross before encountering more freakery. At a bus stop up ahead I could see someone wearing a high visibility vest. Damn. I figured it was an inspector from the Company doing 'random' checks to make sure buses were not running early – which I most certainly was. From a distance it looked like Inspector Harry Potter, a known arsehole famed for his arseholery towards drivers.

But I was wrong. It was arseholery of an altogether different kind. As I pulled into the stop I saw that the man was none other than the Electric Scarecrow – a notorious wacko who goes about Glasgow wearing garishly coloured pyjama-like clothes and is always blasting his head off with headphones turned up to number eleven. As a result, everything he says is SHOUTED.

This evening he came on my bus with ribbons and baubles in his hair and he had also painted henna-like tattoos on his face with dark blue felt tip pen. Definitely the nuttiest punter that a driver could ever hope to get. I was privileged.

He marched on to the bus, flopped his shoulder bag down onto the luggage rack and started fumbling through its zipped pockets for his travel pass. I sat and waited for him. And waited. And waited.

Even through my bandit screen, I could hear his headphones banging out 'River Deep, Mountain High'.

And I waited. And waited.

'YOU'RE TAKING AGES, BIG MAN!!' shouted the 'crow, still fumbling in his bag. He obviously wanted me to drive on while he rummaged for his pass, but I wasn't going anywhere till I'd seen it. He eventually held up a concession pass (wouldn't you just know it?) and I noticed that his hands were encrusted with mud. Had he just come from tending carrots and cabbages at a nearby allotment? No. More likely he had secretly just planted another crop of weed somewhere.

The 'crow did not seat himself. Instead, he stood beside my cab shouting that I was 'TAKING AGES', even whilst stopped at traffic lights. Anyone else would have been ejected for causing such a nuisance but I found him far too entertaining to fling off. A particular delight was when he removed a can of Fanta from his bag, opened it, and drank it through a curly straw.

With his festive attire, effete musical leanings and now with a curly straw in his Fanta, I was beginning to think that he was just possibly a . . .

'DRIVER, YOU'RE MAKING ME LATE FOR MY BOYFRIEND!' he shouted. Query answered. 'HEY DRIVER! IF ANYONE ASKS, TELL THEM I LIKE GETTING SLAPPED RIGHT INTO THE DAFTIES!!'

On we went towards town. A middle-aged woman stood up and tried to open one of the bus windows. But these particular windows were quite difficult to pull open and, even using two hands, she struggled.

'HEY DON'T OPEN THAT WINDOW MISSUS!' shouted the 'crow. 'THE PRESSURE DIFFERENCE! WE'LL ALL BE SUCKED OOT! HA! HA! HA!'

Unbelievably, the woman said, 'Oh!' and sat down.

The Electric Scarecrow Scares a Crow: To me, he's a screwball
I'll always remember – to her he's a screwball she'll never forget.

'HA! HA! HA! AM ONLY KIDDIN' MISSUS! HA! HA! HA! I'VE NOT LAUGHED LIKE THAT SINCE MY

GRANNY CAUGHT HER TIT IN THE MANGLE! HA! HA! HA!'

I was in convulsions in the cab and had to eject a blank ticket to write all this down.

At the bus stop outside Buchanan Street Bus Station the 'crow knocked on my cab door, 'THIS STOP HERE, DRIVER!'

I pulled in and opened the door.

'CHEERS, DRIVER. IF THEY ASK, TELL THEM I'VE LEFT THE COUNTRY!'

'Okay,' I said, but I knew he couldn't hear me.

The Electric Scarecrow stepped off the bus, and for no reason that I could fathom, simply erupted in a convulsive 'HOI!' at the top of his lungs.

The guy is a star.

Well, today had been interesting. Time had been when I would have recoiled at the prospect of junkies, drunkies and luminous nutters crossing my path. But now I knew all the bus routes blindfolded, I was getting rather bored. Anything that broke the monotony, even just one of society's freaks causing a scene on my bus, was actually quite welcome. In fact, as I got a little bolder in the cab, I considered toying with them a bit and was beginning to get a few ideas. I had learned through experience that most lowlifes saw fit to take the piss out of us bus drivers whenever they could, so in future maybe I'd try to get in there first.

19
LUCIANO NEDAROTTI

Thank God! A change of scenery. Today I wasn't going to the squalor of Drumchapel, the roundabout hell of East Kilbride or the rabbit warren of Summerston. Today, it was Bearsden.

Ahh, Bearsden: land of silver BMWs, Mercedes 4x4s and tweedy old ladies with wicker baskets and green wellies. Everyone aspires to live in Bearsden – don't they? And surely there's no delinquency in Bearsden, is there?

As I humped an old Scania single decker down Bearsden Road I came upon three Burberry neds sitting idly on top of a bus shelter like gnomes on a toadstool. They sucked on tobacco leaf and were no doubt regaling each other with exaggerated tales of courage and heroism performed during fist fights of yore, just like gnomes boast about the size of minnows caught on the end of their fishing line. 'Honest, it was THIS big!'

With my approach they jumped down from the bus shelter and stuck out an arm, so I duly pulled in and opened the door.

'All day ticket, driver,' said the first two with a sneer as they clumped aboard. A quick visual check confirmed the validity of their tickets. Hmm, cigarettes and valid bus tickets? Obviously Bearsden neds were neds of some means – Glasgow's nedistocracy.

But not so for the third and final ned. He stood at the

bus stop furiously searching himself like a mongrel with fleas. Clearly the runt of the litter. As the groping continued, his two colleagues Reeboked their way up to the back of the bus where I could hear them talking loudly. 'So, wee Brian grabbed ma heid into a heidlock like this, and shouts *"Ev'rybdy get him!"* But naeb'dy moved! Ha, ha, ha, ha! They all just stood there lookin' at him! "Ev'rybdy get him!" What a wee prick! So I just went like this, *"C'mere yoo!"* – punch! – right in the chops! He falls doon and then I'm like this – boot! – an' he's trying tae cover his mush and get away and . . . hurry up Stevie,' he shouted to the groping ned who was still standing on the pavement with his hands all about himself.

Groping Stevie had, at great length, produced some coins from his pocket. 'Driver, how far could I get for thirty pee?'

'Up to that lamppost.'

'Oh, no! Whit am I goannie dae!' He climbed aboard and addressed the bus, 'Someb'dy give us fifty pee! C'mon! Fifty pee! That's all I need!' Disconcerted passengers looked at each other but nobody threw the dog a bone.

'Ha, ha! Stevie's walking!' added his 'friends'.

As usual, the hapless dope threw himself at the driver's mercy, 'C'mon, driver, just let us oan, eh? C'mon, pal, pleeeeease?'

I could never stand to see such pathetic begging, but the feeling of power over such miserable cretins was undeniably exhilarating – and addictive. I could now sympathize with how God must feel in his heaven: frustratingly superior to all the wretched varmints who tug the hem of his trousers for blessings. So, what to do?

'Can you sing?' I asked the ned.

'Why?' he returned, looking more than a little concerned.

'If you sing 'Twinkle Twinkle Little Star' to my bus, I'll let you on for thirty pee.'

'Oh, no! I'm no doin' that! I've got a really bad singin' voice!'

'Sing it and I'll let you on, don't sing it and you're walking!' I said.

'Alright! Jesus Christ! Driver, you're a bastard, by the way!' Yes, and loving every minute!

'Ladies and gentlemen,' I called to the bus, 'the wee man here is going to sing to you for his ticket.' I then gestured for the ned to commence his lullaby.

'Go on, Stevie!' shouted his mates from the back of the bus.

With a face the colour of beetroot, Stevie began:

'TwinkletwinklelittlestarhowIwonderwhatyouare . . .'

No, no, no! This would not do at all! The pace of his stanza was far too allegro for my liking, and his tortured falsetto whine was making me balk. He was just trying to rattle through it without giving it any feeling. Time for another intervention.

'Stop! Far too fast! You're just speaking it quickly! I want you to make my passengers cry! Start again and sing it properly this time!'

'Fuckin' hell, driver!'

And the poor little bastard did sing it and he sang it well! He sang his little heart out for my bemused passengers. A few times he fumbled the words but I was always there to correct him, pick him up and put his train back on its rails. This was the most fun I'd had since starting the job.

'Ha, ha! Stevie, you're a poof!' shouted his friends from the back seat when it was all over.

'Well done, mate. Take a seat,' I said.

'I can't believe I done that!' said a traumatized Stevie as he walked away up the bus. Neither can I, Stevie, neither can I.

In the spotlight: Luciano Nedarotti gets his laughing gear around a lullaby.

Incoming Radio Message: *This is a lost property call from Central Control. We're looking for a plastic bag containing hair extensions that was left on a bus at the St Enoch Centre about half an hour ago. If you find it on your bus let us know. Control out.*

Hair extensions in a plastic bag??? Since when did hairdressers start doing takeaway? I'll have a perm to go please, with a side order of mullet.

Anyway, I continued humping the Scania towards town when, at Byres Road, (sniff) (sniff), what's this? Someone smoking tobacco leaf on my non-smoking vehicle? But it was more than that. It was a pungent and acrid twang, a bit like...

'Sorry for smoking skunk on your bus, driver,' said Stevie as he came down the bus to get off with his mates. Cheeky little bastard!

'Just be careful, Twinkles,' I said.

In truth, I can fully understand why he had opted for a quick blow of skunk. Firstly to calm his nerves after such an awful vocal rendition of a classic lullaby, but secondly, and more importantly, to get the taste of my big turgid ego out of his mouth.

Back at the depot, Drivers Ubu and Humpty seemed to have made up after their skirmish in the Partick bothy and were suitably impressed by my singing ned. 'Aye, no bad, no bad,' said Ubu. 'Sometimes I get them tae clean up my bus before I let them oan for free. I get them tae clean aff all the beer cans and pizza boxes that manky bastards leave all o'er the floor.'

'That's a good idea,' I said. 'The Tuba would be very grateful to you for that.'

'No, no, no, it's him that makes cleaners grateful!' said Humpty and he pointed to Driver Ubu who quickly got all embarrassed. 'Remember Nasty Nancy, the cleaner?'

'What's all this?' I asked.

'A few years ago, Ubu pumped a cleaner on the back seat of an old Volvo Olympian in the yard. We called her Nasty Nancy,' said Humpty. 'Coz she had a face like a bag full of clam shells.'

'Wait a minute, I wasnae the only one! Fuzzclaw did her too,' came Ubu.

'No, he did that wee fat cleaner with the squint, remember? She was after him for ages. Every time he got back tae the depot with his bus, she would pull him oot the cab and shaft him roon by the engineers' shed.'

'No, that was wee Driver Lip Quiff that did her with the squint!'

'Oh, maybe it was.'

Well, it was as though the domino incident in the bothy had never happened. Over the months, I had actually witnessed several other drivers in the depot engaged in what appeared to be pre-fight verbal exchanges, only to discover they were just saying 'hello'. Perhaps I had read the Ubu vs Humpty situation wrongly. I concluded that the more severe and embittered the altercation between two drivers appeared to be, the longer the drivers had been mates. Ubu and Humpty must have been bosom buddies based on their performance of mutual hate in the bothy. After all, if a mere acquaintance wanted to punch your teeth down your throat, well, that would be considered rather forward.

As these two pals went on discussing which cleaner used to pull which driver out of the cab and pump him round by the engineers shed, I felt quite unsettled. As much as I admired The Tuba, she'd damn well better keep her hands to herself.

20
STONED

'—so, then they put him oan different pills. They were blue pills this time.'

'Did you try to—' I started, but was interrupted mid-sentence as she steamrollered over me.

'He wuz far wurse on them blue pills than he wuz on the red pills. It wuz the side effects mair than an'thin'. Gave him terrible diarrhoea. Terrible, terrible diarrhoea.'

At first I had been happy to offer this little dumpling some polite conversation as we sat at the Clydebank terminus. After all, it's possible that I may have been the only person she spoke to all day. However, when she got started on the side effects of her husband's heart medication, she rattled on like a runaway freight train loaded up with bowling balls.

'Whit a mess! He wuz mingin' a' the time! It was ridiculous!'

'Did you think about getting—' I said, but she cut me off again.

'I says tae him, "You're mingin'! Get back doon tae the doacter right noo! Yer a disgrace!"'

I didn't reply. Every time I tried to offer advice I was scythed down by her sharp whiny voice and pointy pink fingernails. Rather than candidly share her troubles and accept my sympathetic counsel, she selfishly regarded my attentive ear as a convenient colostomy bag for all her domestic offal. I felt dirty and abused.

'Then there's ma youngest boay,' she continued. 'He's no right in the heid.'

I sat with my head in my hands until it was time to leave the terminus. Even then, I had to order her to take a seat and promise not to fire a single verbal bolus at me while I drove. Anyway, we didn't get far before the radio fizzed.

Incoming Radio Message: *This is Central Control to any service passing the Pollok Centre. A Polish driver has pressed his emergency radio button due to a disturbance on his bus, but his English isn't very good. If any driver is passing the Pollok Centre just now could you please check on him and see what's going on. Control out.*

Oh, that's right! Don't bother sending round the police! Just get another bus driver to stop by and risk his own safety by seeing who is trying to carve up the unfortunate Pole. How good does a Pole's English have to be before someone realises he needs urgent assistance?

'Allo? Zis eez Polska driver! Pleeze for you to be help me now! Za nedz! Za nedz! Za Pollok Zeentre nedz! Zey comeski!'

I felt genuine sympathy for the poor Polska. Even more so as I grumbled my way through the despairing depths of Knightswood and observed a little ned with big boots jumping up and down on the roof of an old Austin Metro. His expression of youthful joy was a picture. Almost saintly. It was as though Jesus himself had bestowed a divine blessing on some wretched little Tiny Tim and summoned him forth from his crutch.

And bounce he did. But Tiny Tim's over-exuberance just minded me of the poor Pole's plight at the Pollok Centre.

I imagined a big King Kong sized ape-ned jumping up and down on top of the Polish driver's bus and smashing it right in, real savage-like. Sadly, the Pole is no match for ape-ned in a death-match of strength and agility.

And Jesus said: 'Wretched ned! Cast off thy crutch and bounce thee on high so that all the land may behold my miracle. Hallelujah!'

I left Tiny Tim doing his merry jig on the car roof. In retrospect, I think his violent glee sprang forth from the 75cl bottle of Buckfast in his right hand, not from any anointing by Jesus. Although Buckfast was not directly the work of the Lord, it was made on behalf of the Lord by a bunch of Benedictine monks in Devon. How a child got hold of a bottle of the Lord's 'broon wine' is beyond me, but in any case, the Buckfast monks should maybe think about exercising some social responsibility and bringing out reduced sugar 'Buckfast Toothkind' for the benefit of such young boozers.

Unfortunately, my mind was still haunted by drunken Tiny Tims and brutish ape-neds as I neared the end of my run in East Kilbride. Hopefully the lone ned waiting for me at the Calderwood terminus was neither of these species. As I approached, I saw that his right arm was encased in plaster – a stookie as we call it in Glasgow. Although this limited his potential criminality, his screaming tracksuit committed numerous breaches of the peace on his behalf. It looked more like an angry patchwork quilt, set on fire and extinguished by vomit. The *Cirque de Beelzebub* must be missing a clown.

I opened the doors and Stookie stepped aboard. His thick curly mop of unwashed hair complemented his goofy jester's getup perfectly.

'How much is it intae the toon, driver?' said Stookie, fumbling in his pocket for change.

Whack!

What the . . . ? Before I could blaspheme, my bus was under heavy mortar attack: Whack! Spoing! Boff! Krak! Gwap! Goof! Paff! Donk!

Rocks, stones, bits of wood and other street debris were raining down on my vehicle – all thrown by the hands of unseen bastards from a car park over the wall. I've never driven a bus through an asteroid belt before but this must be just what it's like – *with shields down*.

'Just sit down, mate, I need to move the bus!' I shouted to Stookie.

'Whit?' he said.

'Go and sit down!' I shouted again. 'Stone throwers!'

As if to underline this, a heavy projectile thudded against a side panel and ricocheted back across the street.

'Ha ha ha! They're not stones, driver! They're bricks!' added Stookie.

I hit the gas and made Stookie the Clown stumble up the bus as the hailstorm continued. They were throwing absolutely everything now. But despite the bricks and branches, what I remembered most of all were those little capsules you get inside Kinder eggs that contain the toy. They arced over the wall like grenades, cracked open and bounced along the road in front of me. I could see they had been filled with some kind of liquid. Piss maybe? Beware the ned with sweet tooth and weak bladder.

Having now driven round the corner, I pulled in to inspect the damage. I was soon joined on the pavement by Stookie.

'Ye gonna be waitin' here long mate?' he asked.

'Couple of minutes. I just need to make sure the bus is still in one piece.'

'Good, I'll just have a fag the noo.' He lit up.

As I wandered round the bus, I was astonished to find no serious damage. Apart from a few extra dimples in the side panelling where the larger objects had struck, all the windows were intact – which is what they had been aiming for all along.

'Take it easy, driver, we've all done it!' said Stookie.

'Done what?' I asked.

'Thrown stuff at buses. I've done it mysel'. Stones, cans, bits o' wood, whatever wuz lyin' aroon. Ma favourite wuz mud pies! We used tae hide ahind bushes at the fitba' pitches and lob big mud pies at buses. Ha! Ha! Ha!'

Strange how people begin to appear physically repugnant as they start saying repugnant things. It was only now that I noticed how Stookie's beady eyes were recessed at the back of dark sunken sockets, as though his face had been over-quarried by the numerous hungry insects that no doubt resided in his greasy mop. Beneath those bloodshot bunkers was a nose with the profile of a novelty golf putter, while, lower still, his jutting chin was sloped at the same angle as the nine iron I wanted to clunk over his head as punishment for all his bus crimes.

It's safe to say that his casual comments conjured up all sorts of unpleasant memories in my mind. So I decided to repay him the favour: 'So, how did you break your arm? Was it very *painful*?'

'Aye, I broke it on the front door,' he said with a grimace. Good, I thought, now we'll see if clowns really do weep custard.

'On the front door? Were you trying to punch your way through it or something?'

'Whit? No, I wuz carryin' it. I hud tae carry it fur ma dad.'

'Was that your punishment for firing mud pies at buses?'

'Whit?'

'Was your dad like, "You've been a bad boy, son, go and carry the front door aboot till ye learn not tae fling mud pies at buses"?'

'Whit?'

'Or did he just give you a good thrashing for it instead?'

'Whit?'

He really was quite dim. I bet if you spiked an IQ meter right into his skull, the needle on the gauge would not even quiver. But, sometimes having a low IQ is the only way that delinquents get results, as I was to find out after my meal break.

I walked through the door of the bothy and there was Driver Stingball sitting eating a bag of chips. Although not

THE BLOODBUS

yet back driving buses after his heart scare, they had him working as bothy caretaker during his convalescence. He was currently telling the other drivers in the bothy about the highlight of his stay in the Victoria Infirmary.

'There was a big ward with a smaller ward joined on to it,' said Stingball. 'They put me in the smaller ward so they could keep an eye on me. I was just lyin' in my bed readin' a book when this guy comes wandering in from the big ward. All he was wearing was a filthy T-shirt and a pair of socks! I could see his dick swingin' aboot between his legs as he walked over to my bed. He was just talkin' away to me about this and that as though nothin' was wrong. I just lay there tryin' my best tae talk aboot the weather an' that. Then the nurses clocked him and they were all runin' aboot crazy trying tae cover him up and get him back tae his bed, but he just wouldnae go! It was a mad hoose! You're better aff just snuffin' it!'

He had the whole bothy in hysterics, especially Driver Ubu who almost choked on his bread roll (soft not crispy). Nice to see Stingball back to his old self.

On a full and happy belly, I took an old Volvo single decker up to that ingrowing toenail called Drumchapel. There, three local dumb nuggets were loitering with intent on a roundabout. The first ran up to my bus and made as if to throw a stone at the windscreen, but his clenched fist had been empty all the time. Despite this, my arms flayed spontaneously around the cab like an octopus on electric shock therapy. It's embarrassing but you just can't help it. The neds know it too. It's a classic ruse that works every time.

The other two delinquents were not so forgiving. They attacked from either side of the bus in a pincer movement.

No messing about: *Crunch!* and *Crash!* Two broken windows and glass everywhere. Despite not having the intelligence to hide themselves during the attack, their clinical finishing really did put the East Kilbride neds to shame. Those Kinder egg-throwing fruitcakes really were pitiful in comparison.

With no injuries to report, I contacted control who ordered me just to return to the depot to get another bus. I got back to the yard to find lots of high viz jackets standing around near the depot gatehouse. There was Cloth Ears too, the night shift gaffer. Wonder what he was called out for. Surely not to inspect broken bus windows. I got the feeling that something big was going down tonight.

I drove past them and parked up. Ahead of me, Driver Guy Smiley had also returned to the depot with a smashed window and stepped off his bus.

'Where did yours happen?' asked Guy Smiley.

'Up the Drum,' I replied. 'What about you? East Kilbride by any chance?'

'Aye!' he said. 'Wee bastards! At least nae'bdy got hurt this time. Two weeks ago I got a broken windae in exactly the same place in East Kilbride and had to get an ambulance coz a woman got scudded right in the face. Suspected dislocated jaw.'

Okay, I take back what I said about the East Kilbride fruitcakes. Scoring a direct head shot through a bus window from over a wall requires practice, dedication and skill. Tiger Woods netted a $90 million Nike sponsorship thanks to just such a philosophy. But compared to the commitment and devotion of East Kilbride's bloodthirsty sportsmen, who can serve up an ace-in-yer-face while holding a bottle AND a spliff, I'm afraid the Tiger is still playing crazy golf.

So if he weren't here to inspect broken bus windows, why

was Cloth Ears milling around the bus yard? After some brief enquiries it transpired that a security guard had got raucously drunk in the gatehouse and kept making an arse of himself by staggering into the main depot building every ten minutes to take a piss. Jelly Baby at the desk had taken offence to his high jinks and summoned Cloth Ears to perform a sacking. And Cloth Ears knew no mercy.

21
A GOOD BAMMING

Before the Beginning of All Things, the entire Universe was no larger than a melon. How Mother Nature managed to cram all of Existence into the size of a large tit has had physicists brawling in their labs for years. However, they do agree that it was God's groping hand upon this breast-sized orb that initiated the colossal explosion known as the Big Bang.

Poor God! You can just imagine Him with his face covered in soot, cursing his bad luck and resolving never to fondle anything boob-like or benippled again.

Amazingly, Glasgow's junkies have gone one better than Mother Nature. They can compress an all day ticket down into an infinitely small ball of barely visible pocket fluff.

'I've got an all day ticket, driver,' slurred the dribbling wobble-zombie as he boarded my bus at Calderwood Square in East Kilbride. I was running late and was fearful of being shafted from behind again. But the junkie made damn sure I was even later by searching every pocket in agonizing slow motion.

'Here it is,' he said at last, and produced a crumpled and creased mote of muck-soiled paper that was so impossibly tiny that it defied physics and blew Mother Nature's nipples clean off.

'Thank you,' I grumbled. Even though the ticket was hopelessly unreadable I gave him the benefit of the doubt and decided to let him board. I just wanted to get moving.

'Wait a minute, driver, I've got the other half here somewhere . . .' and another pocket search began. The other half? Oh, dear God.

The hold up attracted the attention of ten or so Young Team that had boarded at East Kilbride bus station. 'Look at him! Look at him! Let's bam him up!' they called to each other as the skinny junkie fumbled.

'Just take a seat, mate,' I said to the wraith. But his chronic display of gratitude claimed only my pity: 'Nice one, mucker. Cheers, mate. Thanks pal. You're a gentleman. You're a gentleman. God bless you. God bless you, son.' He measured out his words so slowly and moved his mouth so slightly that there must surely have been a nettle leaf under his tongue. Given a hand-puppet he would have made a master ventriloquist.

He staggered up the bus like a man pulling himself through waist-deep treacle and flopped down beside a terrified old woman. Immediately after pulling away from the bus stop, the Young Team began shouting and taunting the junkie from their back seat eyrie.

'Hey, junkie! Hey, smack heid!'

'Fuck off, ya wee bastards!' returned the junkie, shouting through his nose. The little old woman's face was a picture. However, his retaliation only encouraged the Young Team to up-the-ante by breaking into song:

Let's all laugh at smack head, lets all laugh at smack head, na na na na, na na na na!

The junkie stood up and faced the hectoring mob, 'Hey! I'm no a smack heid! I'm a fuckin' wino!'

'Ha! Ha! Ha! Ha!' came the Young Team.

Well, what was he expecting from them? After all, saying, 'Hey! I'm not a maggot, I'm a grub!' won't make any difference when you're being slobbered up by the tongue of a hungry Aardvark.

On it went. As I approached the Kingsgate Retail Park, the junkie snapped under the weight of the Young Team's incessant jibes. He hobbled up to the back of the bus shouting, 'Come on then! I'll take the fuckin' lot of you on! Right now!'

I immediately pulled the bus in to the side of the road and opened the doors. According to Chucklemumble, fights usually spill off the bus and on to the pavement which allows the driver to shut the doors and get away. With the Young Team's numerical advantage, I figured this fight would be over pretty quickly.

It wasn't. In fact, it didn't really get started. The Young Team were in such hysterics that every time the scrawny junkie came within punching range, they simply pushed or kicked him away. The rawboned doper would then fall down, crawl away, pull himself up and try again – but every time he would end up on the floor.

The only people that fled the bus were a few panic-stricken passengers and the terrified old lady. One brutish skinhead looked at me accusingly as he left the bus and said, 'That's a shocker that you're allowing that to happen on your bus, driver! I'm waiting for the next one.'

Once again, responsibility for society's ills was shat on my doorstep. It would have all been over by the time the police turned up anyway, and there was no way I was going to risk trying to sort it out myself – I drive a bus, I don't referee scum fights. I just sat and watched the poor junkie tumble to the floor, get up again, attack, and tumble to the floor once more. He really wasn't making progress at all. At least a housefly banging it's head against a glass window can be put out of its misery with a flick of *The Times*.

At long last the junkie relented and came back down the bus to take his seat, spitting curses at the howling Young Team. Verbal exchanges continued all the way to the Cathkin roundabout where the junkie came down the bus to get off.

'You've got a bus full of bastards, driver!' said the druggy.

I pulled in and opened the door. He stepped off the bus and took a few seconds to get his bearings.

'Let's get aff here and follow him! Aye! C'mon we'll bam him up some more! Lets bam him up tae fuck!' said the Young Team and came marching down the bus. The junkie saw them and began hobbling away at speed.

The dopester had a curious, low, short-step hobble as though he were bound by a set of heavy leg irons. Such old-school punishment may befit a man capable of the treachery and misdeed required to fund a smack habit. Indeed, medieval justice may be a more effective long-term treatment for his drug addiction than giving him a flat in Cathkin and a daily shot of methadone.

A Good Bamming: If following a junkie around Cathkin and laughing at him keeps neds off my bus then I might start dealing.

I didn't hang around to watch the rest of this Benny Hill chase due to timetable constraints. Looking on the bright side, at least I got the junkie and the Young Team off the bus. But I couldn't ignore the stench of piss that lingered.

Decided not to bother with an incident report when I got back to the depot. Why should I waste my time at the end of a long shift on account of a miserable junkie and a few neds? After all, there was a nip of Glenfiddich waiting for me in the house. Yum!

But, having now returned to the depot, I noticed a police car sitting in the yard. That only happened when something very nasty had taken place. Usually a stabbing or vicious assault. There was Driver Fuzzclaw milling around outside the depot office with a fag. If anyone knew what was going on, he would. After the Oompa Loompa had taken the cash box out of my bus, I parked up and spoke to the 'claw.

'How come the filth are in tonight?' I asked.

'They're here aboot Driver Gollum,' he said.

'Oh, what's he done now?'

'It's not what he's done. It's what someone did tae him. He got intae a fight wi' a gang o' neds coz they were ridin' aboot on his bus, carryin' on and drinking Buckie and all that. They ended up at the Greenhills terminus, etchin' the windaes and writin' graffiti everywhere, so Gollum gets oot his cab and starts shoutin' the odds the way he does.'

'Yeah, I've seen him in action.'

'The neds all just set aboot him and knocked him oot cold on the floor of his ain bus.'

'Jesus! Is he alright?'

'Nope. He woke up concussed and covered in blood and the neds had scarpered. Had to go to hospital. But get this

– Jelly Baby's in there behind the desk moanin' coz there was no one on standby tae cover the shift.'

'What? The prick!' I cussed.

'Aye, make nae mistake, you're nothin' maire than a number in here,' said Fuzzclaw.

'Was Gollum on a camera bus? Any CCTV?'

'No, it was an old Olympian and the radio wasnae working either. Just as well they never nicked his mobile phone aff him so he could call for help. The stupid bastard should have just stayed in his cab.'

'Aye, he was always bragging about being the hard man and sorting trouble out on his bus,' I said.

'He's a nutter. That's how tae end up deid in this joab!' said Fuzzclaw.

I for one did not intend ending up 'deid'. Especially not for these slave-driving buggers who saw fit to send us out in old, barely-legal vehicles with inoperative radios. Later, as I swirled the ice around my tumbler of Glenfiddich, I wondered just how long I was going to last in the job. Up until now, I figured there were two paths to freedom from this purgatory – resign or get fired. But, tonight, Driver Gollum made me realise there was a third. And the third one hurt.

22

WHITE CHOCOLATE

Stingball was still on caretaker duty in the Partick bothy and had brought in a porn DVD for our entertainment. I think there is a time and place for porn but it's definitely not the bus drivers' bothy when you're on a break. Money shots and deep throat really put you off your Pot Noodle. I was actually quite glad when a scraggy new female driver, Hippogonk, came into the bothy and made him switch it off.

'But you'll like it, it's got lesbian bits in it,' protested Stingball.

'Just coz I'm a bus driver doesn't make me a lesbian!' shouted Hippogonk. 'Switch it off!'

There were boos all round.

Having been out of the loop for a few weeks, Stingball then asked to be updated on who had left the job and who'd been fired. There were four or five names mentioned, but no one I'd heard of. Then Driver Ticklemop recounted a classic tale of how one particular driver came to grief a few years ago.

'Remember that manky bastard wi' the club foot and the honey pot hand that used to get on roon' aboot Paisley Road West?' started Ticklemop. 'He used tae carry his bus fare aboot in his mooth, and come on tae yer bus and just spit the money into yer coin tray. Noo, this is back in the days when we used tae handle cash so we had tae count it all oot by hand. It was really rotten! But one time, he gets on Big Billy's bus and spits oot his money into the coin tray, but Billy says, "Here! That's fuckin' disgusting! I've had enough o' this!" so he prints a ticket, licks it, and slaps it to the guys forehead! Ha! Ha! Ha! He got kicked oot straight away for that!'

After I picked myself up off the ground I asked if there had been any word about Gollum.

'Aff on the thick!' lisped Chucklemumble who had just come into the bothy. 'I thpoke tae him on the phone lath nite. He had tae have a brain thcan in hothpital. Thed he might not be comin' back at all. He thounded ath though he'd had enough of the joab.'

He wasn't the only one. As I finished my Pot Noodle and headed out to the relief point, I felt myself tensing up with anxiety before my bus had even arrived. I almost bit some poor bugger's head off at the bus stop just for asking me when the next bus was due. It was having to deal with drunkies, junkies, muppets and neds every day that was bringing out a side of me I really didn't like. When every punter is only a word away from an angry snap, and every motorist only an indicator flash away from an irate honk, it's impossible not to be affected. It really gets to you. Gollum was right to bail out. That clunk on his head obviously brought with it a moment of clarity.

After picking up my bus, I distracted myself with a bit of punter watching. As ever, I was not disappointed, for straight on to my bus walked The King himself. He got on at Dalmarnock Road as I headed into the city centre. Everything was there: the quiff, the shades, the side burns, the open neck shirt with gold chain, the curly top lip, the big belt buckle and ooh! That swagger! Thank goodness, I needed a bit of cheering up. But why would a man supposed to be in hiding give himself away like this? Because he's a cunning bastard! Who better to disguise himself as than the very last person anyone would ever expect him to disguise himself as. Himself! We'd naturally just associate him with all the other nutter Elvis impersonators out there. In a sort of 'I'm Spartacus!' way. Unfortunately, this being a rainy Glasgow evening, The King didn't look 'All Shook Up' so much as, well, a bit bedraggled.

He held up his hands to everyone as if to say, *No photographs or autographs!* as though the murmurs of amusement and pity from soggy commuters were in fact roars of adoration to his rock 'n' roll ears. Despite there being plenty of seats available, he preferred the limelight and stood at the front of the bus for the whole journey, smiling at all the passengers. Everyone smiled back. Even da white hip hop home-boys playing gangsta rap through their mobile phones at the back of the bus seemed fairly entertained and begged him to sing. As we approached Bridgeton, I was really hoping he would. There were a few beasty girls from Rutherglen he could have serenaded with a rendition of 'Hound Dog', but sadly, it didn't come.

Instead, my bus was treated to a different sort of cabaret. As I turned the corner at Bridgeton cross, I noticed two police cars and one police van parked up on the pavement. Officers were dragging a short, stocky, raggedy man out of the Liquor Barn and threw his yelling face down onto the concrete. Six cops piled on top of him with cuffs at the ready as he shouted and kicked and flailed. A female officer wrestled what looked like a leather belt out of his right hand.

A leather belt? Okay, so we don't allow free ownership of guns in this country, but my God there has to be more fearsome weaponry to use in an off-licence hold up than a friggin' leather belt. A knife? A screwdriver? A table leg even? Unless, of course, the belt had an altogether different purpose. Maybe he was using it Indiana Jones style to whip bottles of whisky off the top shelf while the shop assistant's attention was diverted. Just like a chameleon can shoot its sticky tongue out of its head at 22 kilometres per second, a thirsty Glasgow drunk can whip a bottle of Johnny Walker off the top shelf as though it were a tasty cricket snoozing on a branch.

Elvis stepped off the bus still grinning broadly and stood watching the drama unfolding in front of him. I really don't know why he was looking so smug, especially when you consider how he allegedly met his end. Yes, when you consider that the King of Rock and Roll checked out by having a cardiac arrest while sitting on the potty trying to pass one of his fried peanut butter and banana sandwiches, it really did make being clobbered by the law and pounded into the back of a van seem like an almost tranquil farewell. It also made his 1958 classic 'Wear My Ring Around Your Neck' somewhat ironic, especially if you were the coroner.

A wee muppet stepped on to the bus. 'Jesus Christ! It takes six o' them tae get him intae the back o' a van! Six o' them!' Her impatience with the police's handling of the raggedy man made her sound as though she could have performed the arrest herself, single-handed.

She was probably right too. With almost one in ten Glasgow women having admitted cutting, bruising or even breaking bones during altercations with their male partners, I'd say the raggedy man got off lightly. In fact, the police should get rid of those silly extendable batons and arm themselves properly with flesh-ripping Glasgow attack-muppets such as the yappy little growler addressing me.

Indiana Drunk: 'Alright sweet
o' Babysham from the bottom
bottom. (WHIP) (CLANK) T
by the way. One o' yer shelve
the drunk, a passing policem
A policeman who just happen
on the en

Da hip hop homies stayed
Maryhill Road playing their
the Elephant and Bugle pu
a cadaverous old lady on.
tufts of hair grew prodigiou
unruly foliage escaping thr
abandoned greenhouse, and
more fragile than a soggy I

'Driver, I've been asking
fumbling in her handbag f
'Yes?' I asked.
'What is white chocolat
'Eh?'
'I've been asking everybo
and nobody seems to kno

rt, aye, just give us a
elf. Aye, that's it, right
t noise wiz nothin' tae
must be loose.' Unfortu
happened to see his ev
' to have a vicious atta
f a chain . . .

on the bus all t
gangsta rap nonse
I pulled into a h
he was almost a
ly from every fa
ugh the broken
er pale, transluc
izla.
everybody toda
her concession

?'

ly what white cl
! Do you know,

a

it

sp
ag
I
bu

fa

sp

ne

nec
it
the

nec
be
o' y

just
bec

the white chocolate homies actually said to the ned's dad to give themselves away on the phone so obviously.

(RING) (RING)

'Hello?'

'Yo, yo, yo, yo, yo! Wassup, pops? We's comin' at ya wit da attitude from da club an' shit! Yo hear what i'm sayin', ya fuck? Say what? I wanna touch dat thang! Don't ya pussy wit me, gold digga bitch! You ain't never gonna know who we is! We's slap yo booty!'

(CLICK)

23

SPILLAGE, GROT, RUMPLE AND FREAK

At the Drumchapel terminus I sat and watched a murder of crows hopping around and squabbling on a pile of rubble where the council had knocked down some derelict flats. I don't know what they were fighting over but it sure must have been tasty.

A **murder** of crows. My favourite collective noun.

That got me thinking. What would be the collective nouns for the drunkies, junkies, muppets and neds that I ferry about on my bus every day? Some suggestions:

A **spillage** of drunks.

A **grot** of junkies.

A **rumple** of muppets.

A **freak** of neds.

Maybe there had been a **grot** of junkies holed up in those derelict flats when the council's wrecking ball came through the wall. True martyrs to their habit, they decided to go down with their skag. Or, more likely they were just too wasted and kept banging into each other as they made for the door.

But it's all good news for the crows. As far as they're concerned, juicy junkie limbs beat skinny earthworms any day. In Drumchapel, hungry crows follow demolition trucks like seagulls follow fishing boats. Easy pickings.

Mind you, junkies are probably not half as tasty as today's slop shop special from Chowder Chops – chicken curry

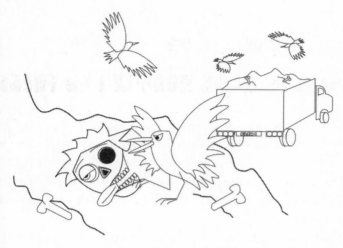

Crow's feet around the eyes makes anyone look past their best.

with the same consistency as play dough. Really hits the spot.

'I can recommend the curry,' I said when I dragged my expanding gut past Jelly Baby.

There was no reply.

'Really sticks to your ribs.'

Still no reply. Normally he's quite the chatterbox at the front desk, but on this occasion he was just staring into space with a glazed look in his eye. Eventually he just shook his baldy, knuckled head.

'What's up?' I asked.

'Another driver's just been fired and I've got no one to cover the shift. How am I supposed to keep the wheels turning when they keep firing drivers? I've just about had it!'

'Who's been fired this time?'

He explained. Apparently there had been a spate of window smashings at Fernhill in Rutherglen and a team of inspectors were dispatched in a car to sit and covertly watch the neds. However, Driver Ubu was seen driving past the neds in his bus, shouting abuse at them and giving the middle finger so they would go nuts and break his windows. He would then be able to get out of service for half an hour. I distinctly remembered Ubu saying that I had been a 'lucky bugger' to get a broken window previously, and now I knew he really meant it. But it still seemed a bit harsh to sack a driver just for trying to incite trouble. But Jelly Baby assured me it got worse.

The inspectors decided to follow Ubu to the terminus and observe him instead of the neds. They had been shocked to witness Driver Ubu get off his bus, look around for a suitable boulder and crunch it through one of his very own bus windows. He had then radioed the control room to say that those terrible neds had broken yet another bus window and that he needed to return to the depot. As soon as he stepped off the bus and walked into the depot office he was sacked.

This was a classic! I could sense the birth of another legendary firing tale that would equal Ticklemop's story of the driver who was kicked out for sticking the bus ticket to someone's forehead. So, that was Gollum and Ubu gone. Not very good for morale, but it provided much fodder for the gossipmongers of the bothy. Ironically, it was their humorous recounting of such bus driving tales around the bothy campfire that gave us the chuckle we needed to go out and face the rest of the shift. Other drivers' misery was our medicine.

Anyway, I left the crows at the Drumchapel terminus and

immediately came upon a whole **freak** of young neds playing football in the street. After a bit of 'Let's line up in the middle of the road and not let the bus past,' they did what every group of neds does with a football – boot it against the side of the bus.

They ALWAYS do it. It's an in-built reflex, and it's not a little tap either, it's a full force BLAST. Now I know where Barnes Wallis got the idea for his 'Bouncing Bomb'. But even then he had to fill it up with seven tons of RDX explosive just to get the same effect.

But today, fate decided that I should have the last laugh. Sure enough, one of the little pricks blasted the ball against my bus, but the ball ricocheted off the side panel, hit a fence, bounced back towards the bus, rolled into the gutter under the bus, and well, I just couldn't help myself! I steered a little bit to the left and ... BANG! ... what a noise a Mitre Mouldmaster makes when it bursts!

The blast made the explosion of Mount Krakatoa seem like a benign caterpillar fart as nearby residents came to their windows to see what was going on. All they saw was a freak of five glum-faced neds standing in the street gazing down, misty eyed, at the flaccid remains of their injection-moulded football of death. Oh! And one laughing bus driver!

Well, that kept a smile on my face all day. Nothing could bring me down after that. Even when I went for my break and accidentally walked in on Driver Jolly Mop taking a dump in an unlocked toilet cubicle in the depot, I merely nodded and winked as he flailed to keep himself on the bowl. The day was mine.

But the piece de resistance was still to come ...

There was a weeping hag sitting in the bus shelter at Jamaica Street holding on to her stomach. I figured that the fresh Jackson Pollock at her feet was hers, having risen unbidden from her wretched guts. Everyone seemed to be ignoring her and her pathetic moans, but as I came to a halt, a **spillage** of drunks from the direction of the Crystal Palace bar came to offer assistance.

Despite the hag's hellish disposition I am never one to mock the Lord's work, so I opened the doors to see if she or her new friends wanted on. One of the tubbier members of the spillage was now sitting next to the hag in the bus shelter with his arm around her.

The tragedy of that friendly act was this: the hag may have believed that this cuddly blobster was going out of his way to comfort her in her moment of need. A selfless and sympathetic gesture in our usually 'me first' society. But I knew the truth. I know the mind of men and this particular man had the look of a sexual vulture. This was the worst case of beer goggles I had ever seen.

Here was a vulnerable female in a depressed and weakened state, but Mr Blobby was eyeing her with all the compassion of a hyena tracking a wounded gazelle. Granted, the hag was nothing more than walking carrion, but when a sexual scavenger like Mr Blobby is on the prowl, no amount of bile on the pavement could throw him off the scent of a good dead sheep.

Until, of course, I closed the doors. Then he was up and on his feet. (BANG) (BANG) (BANG) 'Driver! Let me oan!' I opened the door and Mr Blobby stepped on, but turned round to the hag one last time.

'You gonna be alright?' he asked.

The hag nodded.

'You sure?'

The hag nodded.

'D' you want ma phone number?'

The hag shook her head.

'Can I have your phone number?'

The hag shook her head again. The oaf had been denied! Turned down by a Glasgow hag! No meat tonight for Mr Blobby! Ha, ha, ha! A dejected Mr Blobby sat at the very back of the bus amongst a dozen discarded fish and chip wrappers. I saw that he kept leaning over, picking up wrappers and picking through them. What the hell was he up to?

At the bottom of Bath Street the King's Theatre had just belched out the largest **rumple** of muppets I had ever seen. The whole spectrum of muppetry was represented, from little smiling ballers to tall scowling rakes.

'Baaahhh!' shouted Mr Blobby and threw a rolled up fish and chip wrapper down the bus. He then turned his attention to another wrapper on the floor. I still didn't understand what he was up to, but on the CCTV screen he looked like a pot bellied pig snuffling for truffle.

'Good evening, driver!' said a couple of happy little muppets as they boarded with even happier hats. Wait a minute, no one ever says *Good evening, driver!* These two were obviously still in Polite Society Mode having just been mincing about with respectable people during the show. Unfortunately, Polite Society Mode doesn't work well on a bus at this time of night. Not with my clientele.

'Two to Queen Margaret Drive, please.'

I printed their tickets.

'Thank you very much.'

But before they could tear the tickets off the ticket machine, Mr Blobby bellowed forth once more: 'Baaahhh! NAE FUCKIN' CHIPS IN THAT ONE NEITHER!' and threw another crumpled wrapper down the bus. The paper cauliflower came to rest a short distance away from the

*Bombs away: When 'Polite Society Mode' meets a brute's wrath,
there can be only one victor.*

muppets' shiny shoes and walking sticks. The expression of
shock on their ashen faces was priceless, like someone had
scudded each of them in the kisser with a loaded talc puff.

So that's what Mr Blobby was doing all along – *looking for
leftovers!* Being denied his prey on Jamaica Street just made
him realise the full extent of his voracious appetite.

Oh well, like the crows in Drumchapel always say: 'If you
can't get hot meat, make do with someone else's remains'.

24
NIGHT OF THE LIVING NED

The neds were in a funny mood tonight. As I stood at the relief point in that noxious yeast infection known as Whiteinch, I could hear fearful shouts and screams coming from the cheerless back streets nearby. With police vans going up and down I reckoned there must have been some serious ned on ned action going on in the shadows. Most likely a Buckfast fuelled turf war, not that there's anything worth fighting over in Whiteinch.

Despite living in a fairly civilised Western society, the peasant class will always find something to fight over. At least when their Grandfathers were neds over half a century ago they had something meaningful to fight over, i.e. Europe. But what have today's neds in Whiteinch got to fight over? Let's see, there's a vandalised phone box, an abandoned sideboard and an upturned bath. Quite a prize.

Wearing my bus driver's uniform I was just asking to be caught in the crossfire. I had already received a mouthful of abuse from a group of neds on their way to the front line and feared that worse was to follow. Every war inflicts so called 'collateral damage', and with me wearing my high viz vest I was simply inviting stray bullets. Thankfully, Driver Fuzz Claw turned up on time with the bus so I could get the hell out of there.

'Have you heard the latest?' said Fuzz Claw. 'Jelly Baby's spat the dummy!'

'Spat the dummy?'

'Aye! He went nuts at The Manager coz they kept firing drivers and then put more pressure on him tae get shifts covered. He was always fighting a losing battle in there. I think Ubu smashing his own window just pushed him over the edge.'

'So, what did The Manager do? Fire him?' I asked.

'No, just demoted him. The Manager said, "With an attitude like that I'll have you back on driving duty!" Then Jelly Baby said, "Fine! Shove it! I'll happily go back to driving first thing Monday morning!" But The Manager said, "No! I'll have you back driving tomorrow morning!" Jelly Baby said, "Fine then! See you tomorrow morning!" and walked oot! Ha! Ha! Ha!'

So, Jelly Baby was one of us again. A mere driver. A grunt. He'd laughed at me when I complained that Stingball had tailed me all the way to Clydebank. I wondered if his attitude to a shafting would still be so nonchalant when he was on the receiving end. I couldn't wait to find out.

I climbed into the cab and bolted off down the street looking for anything remotely Jelly Baby shaped to tail. But at the very next stop I was hailed by a skinny ned and his rotund nedette. When I opened the doors I noticed that the ned had a nasty gash on his forehead. Blood was running down the side of his face and congealing on his chin. Probably a sad casualty from the Battle of the Bath. My passengers all gasped at once and there was much muppet-twittering.

Despite their horrific appearances, I couldn't help but compare them both to a confectioner's shop window. With the ned's pale face and bloody dribbles you could stick a spoon in his head and have yourself a convincing knickerbocker glory. His podgy nedette on the other hand, in her white tracksuit, was a large meringue, yet her face seemed all knotted and folded like a grumpy croissant or leering loaf. So bulbous, it was surely the devil himself who rolled the dough in some perverse patisserie.

'Excuse me!' I shouted as they both shuffled their way up the bus.

'Whit?' snarled the nedette.

'That cut on his head—'

'It's just a wee one, he'll be alright, just let him stay oan the bus!'

'I'm sure he will be alright, but I don't want him dribbling all over my seats.'

'Fuck's sake driver! Just let him stay oan! He'll be alright!'

'At least give him this . . .' and I fished out a packet of tissues from my bag and threw them up the bus. I always carried a packet of tissues in my bag, not for my snotty nose or for any sins of impurity but for exactly this purpose – to give to people who come on my bus with bloody faces so they can clean themselves up. It did happen from time to time.

A few stops later, a wee bald man-muppet came down the bus to get off. He knocked my bandit screen. 'Driver!' he said. Here we go, he'll probably bend my ear for allowing blooder boy and his foldy-faced girlfriend to board.

'Yes?' I said, and prepared for the onslaught.

'Driver, do you know this bus has got a broken window?'

'Eh? How can it have a broken window?'

'Wee boys were throwing stones at the bus up in Drumchapel before you started driving it. The glass in one of the windows is all shattered.'

'And no one told the previous driver about it?'

'No, but it was quite loud when it happened. We all thought he knew there was a broken window.'

Damn that Fuzz Claw! I bet he did know about it but being a lazy bastard left me to do the dirty work of transferring angry punters on to another bus, not to mention the paperwork at the depot. The swine!

I put on my hazard warning lights, got out my cab to have a look and sure enough, the glass in the emergency exit was all shattered. Luckily it hadn't fallen out yet.

Time for the announcement that all punters hate but one I was beginning to like more and more: 'I'm afraid this bus has to go 'Not In Service' back to the depot. I'll wait here until the next bus comes along so you don't have to wait at the side of the road.'

'No! (THUD) No! (THUD) No! (THUD) No! (THUD)' squawked the apish meringue girl as she stamped the floor with her feet.

I turned to face the bellowing meringueutan. 'No?'

'No!' she yelled once more. 'If this bus can go frae Drumchapel doon tae Whiteinch wi' a broken windae, then you can take us frae Whiteinch in tae the toon wi' a broken windae!'

'Well, what if we go over a bump and all that glass falls out on top of someone?'

'Listen! This bus is due in the toon in fifteen minutes! Get back in there and start driving! You should be keepin' tae yer timetable!'

'Nope, this bus is going back to the depot.'

Other disgruntled passengers began leaving the bus to get away from the mad meringueutan who was now flailing her blood-smeared hands about.

'Stay oan the bus, everybody! He's gonnae take us! He's gonnae take us!' she whined.

'No he's not,' I said.

'Tell him for Christ's sake!' she shouted to her blood-soaked companion, looking for backup. But the soiled ned was preoccupied with more important issues, such as finding his last remaining cigarette.

'Aw no!' shouted the bloody ned after groping in his tracksuit pocket. 'Ya bastard! I've snapped the fag in ma trackie bottoms! That was ma last wan!' He angrily crumpled both cigarette halves and threw a spray of tobacco leaf down the bus.

By now, most passengers had left the bus and were standing at the bus stop waiting for the next bus. The meringueutan and her lanky ned finally got up and marched off the bus. But the seething ape now targeted her anger at the poor wee man-muppet who initially brought the broken window to my attention.

Knickerblooder Gory and Meringueutan: Straight from Hell's Kitchen.

'If that wee baldy prick had kept his mooth shut we would still be goin'!'

'Calm doon!' said blood boy.

'Hey!' shouted the meringueutan to the man-muppet who was scuttling away across the street. 'Could ye no keep yer fuckin' mooth shut?'

'Calm doon!' shouted blood boy once again. 'There's cops goin' aboot tonight. You'll end up gettin' lifted again. Think aboot your weans! Think aboot Jordan and Dominique!'

Jordan and Dominique! Ha, ha! Belter! It didn't seem to do much for her, but the mention of Jordan and Dominique sure made me feel better. Or maybe it was just the knowledge that Jelly Baby had come back down to earth with a bump. I had a score to settle with him, and I'm pretty sure many other drivers did too. It was only a matter of time.

25

LEMMINGS

The rain hadn't stopped all day. Just as I was finishing the safety checks on my bus in the yard, I spied a sodden but familiar figure wearing civilian dress scurrying through the depot gates. He was carrying a bulging black binliner which meant only one thing – he was handing back his uniform. I caught up with him just before he got to the depot office.

'What happened? Are you leaving?' I asked.

'Thacked!' cursed Chucklemumble.

'You're kidding! What for?'

'Accthidentally hit my wing mirror on a buth thtop pole.'

'Christ! Is that all?'

'Aye, but the glath in the mirror broke and it wath the thecond thime I did it in thix month. Inthtant thacking. Theh! Theh!'

That just seemed crazy. Here was a driver with over twenty years service kicked to the kerb for accidentally misjudging his swing into a couple of bus stops. Every driver smacked their wing mirror off a bus stop pole at some point, usually when a punter was distracting you by asking some silly question. 'When's the last 47 next Thursday night, driver?' Whack! Most of the time the glass didn't break, but you just needed to be unlucky a couple of times in quick succession, and it's hasta la vista.

'You've got to go to the Union and appeal against this!' I said.

'Yeth, I will do. We'll thee what happenth. I'll thee you later,' he said, and into the office he went.

'Good luck, mate,' I said and walked back across the yard to my bus now feeling quite angry. Another nail had just been beaten into the coffin of staff morale. It just seemed like yesterday that Chucklemumble was giving me advice on how to survive as a bus driver. Over the months, he had enlightened me with all the tricks of the trade – how to get out of trouble, how to save yourself when they tried to finger you. But, for all his little tricks, he couldn't save himself when it came to it. Twenty years service and nothing to show for it but a soggy black bin bag.

I climbed into the saddle and left the depot. For a good hour or two I had quite a complex about smacking my own wing mirror off stationary objects and was compelled to swing only half way into bus stops. Safe to say I didn't make any friends with the vehicles behind me who couldn't get past. I just let them honk.

The roads were much quieter later on when I hauled an overloaded night bus all the way down Paisley Road West to that skanky skid mark known as Linwood. The singing, chanting and screaming of seventy alcohol-raddled goofers seemed to intermingle and interweave, forming a ragged tapestry of unholy babble in the air. It was quite stressful and felt like carrying a heavy sack of coal on my back. Only the Tamanac tribesmen of South America can achieve such a frenzied climax when they get high on Yopo snuff and try to resurrect demons.

And the demons cometh.

All the unrestrained wailing of my passengers must indeed have disturbed the deepest shadows of the Underworld, because waiting for me at Cessnock Underground was a foul ogress of untamed villainy. As though scorched by the flames of hell, her wiry skeleton was hung with orange, leathery flesh, her head was a round lump of cheddar and her nose was a shiny doorknob of finely polished brass. Hell fire or tanning salon – either way she was a flambéed whore.

'Know where I'm goin'?' she said with a Marlboro croak.

'No,' I said.

'Helen Street polis station! Maximum security lock up, man! Ha! Ha! Ha!'

Her gaping mouth was an insidious nicotine stained rut which revealed a jagged dental wasteland that reminded me of opening a box of broken eggs. In fact, her entire oral cavity was an ode to back alley bric-a-brac, truly a joyous hymn to the kind of scattered remains that rain down after a gas explosion.

'It's £2.10 night fare,' I said.

'Discount for cash? Ha! Ha! Ha!'

She plopped some coins into the slot, but without waiting for her ticket, she frisked away up the bus and started chicken dancing with standing passengers. It would have taken every last Tamanac tribesman frenzying at their very best to summon such a ghoulish spectre. But just as I was about to close the doors and move off, I noticed another figure in the shadows. A black guy was standing at the bus stop counting out change. Eventually he stepped on to the bus, threw 80p into the coin slot and said, 'Paisley.'

'I'm afraid it's £2.10 to Paisley. Night fare.'

He pulled out a five pound note. 'You got change?'

'Exact fare only. These buses don't give change.'

'Hey! Come on, man! Just let me on?'

'You'll need to find an extra £1.30 from somewhere,' I said.

'Please, man! Please!'

Orangina, the chicken dancing ogress, became annoyed

with the delay and decided to intervene. In a storm of gristly giblets, she frisked back down the bus and got right in the black guy's face. 'GET YER MONEY OOT!' she pecked. But the man just looked down forlornly at his fiver. She tried again, this time clapping for emphasis. 'GET (clap) YER (clap) MONEY (clap) OOT!'

Still the man stood, looking down at his fiver. I think he was quite stunned by Orangina Ogress and the scorching knives of her orange stare.

'GET (clap) YER (clap) FUCKIN' (clap) MONEY (clap) OOT!'

Call of the Ogress: 'Get yer money oot!'

The man of colour eventually bottled it, 'Fuck you, man!' he exclaimed and ran off the bus looking quite mentally rodgered. Shame really because I was actually going to let him on. I wasn't even going to make him sing 'Twinkle Twinkle Little Star', didn't have time for that, I just wanted him to beg a bit first.

'Did you hear that language? Ha! Ha! Ha!' said Orangina Ogress, her laugh crackling like splintered wood. Then someone's mobile phone rang up the back, 'Ooh!' she whooped. 'Whose ringtone's that? That's fuckin' gallus!' and off she went to investigate.

Fortunately, I had unloaded most of my anarchic cargo by the time I got to Paisley Cross. That sack of coal on my back had lost much of its boisterous bulk and was now just a plain old packet of barbeque briquettes. And by Linwood it was no more threatening than a bag of cat litter.

But, just as I was beginning to relax: BUZZZZZZZZZ.

An alarm buzzer in my cab told me that the emergency door had just been opened. I checked the CCTV monitor and saw two young blokes at the back of the bus, one of them was hanging half way out the emergency exit.

Ahhhh! Lemmings! This always gave me a chuckle!

The bloke shouted, 'Whaaaaa!' and leapt off the bus. Although not quite a Fosbury Flop, the guy just crumpled when he hit the tarmac, then rolled and rolled and rolled along behind the bus. Great to watch.

I figured his colleague was staying on the bus so I hammered the accelerator pedal down hard in order to flip the emergency door shut. But instead of the expected *clunk*, all I got was a rather disappointing *thwap*. It appeared that Lemming No.2 did actually intend to make the suicidal leap and was half way out of the door when I performed my little door closing trick. He must have taken the full force of the emergency door right in the kisser because he immediately fell down on to the road backwards and slammed the back of his head on the tarmac. Superb!

When I was still a new start, I used to slow the bus down for lemmings. Not anymore. In fact, now I speed up, especially tonight because I was angry about Chucklemumble being bagged on a whim. If my passengers wanted to kill themselves then I wanted a ringside seat. I was quite happy to let the little shits tumble out the back of my moving vehicle with all the nonchalance of a horse rolling hot balls of doo-doo out its rear end. Like a quick-bowelled stallion I didn't even furrow my brow for the occasion. With a swish of my tail, I had dropped two steaming lumps of manure in the middle of Bridge Street tonight and then galloped off, leaving them to the flies.

Bon appetit!

26
FIRESTARTER GETS FRAGGED

Although 'bus' and 'banana skin' both start with the same letter, they are dissimilar in every other possible way, right? Wrong! At least, not if you're a Glasgow muppet. Over the course of this year, I've seen an assortment of hapless muppets falling on to the bus, falling off the bus and getting clobbered by bits of bus falling on top of them, but, until today, I've never seen a muppet going down merely because of a bus's *aura*.

I was waiting for my bus at Anniesland Cross during the evening rush and had my MP3 player turned right up to drown out the sound of manic drivers trying to honk each other to death. As I dum-de-dummed my way through 'Lucy In The Sky', a stout little muppet wrapped up like an Eskimo made a frantic hobble for a bus that was just about to pull away from the stop. In a melee of stubby limbs, she flapped towards the bus with all the determination of a bloated turtle pulling itself up a beach to lay eggs.

However, the driver of the bus had no idea of the muppet's frantic flight and hit the door close button just at the crucial moment when she tried to step aboard. At first I thought she was going to get trapped in the doors, but she managed to stop herself just as they slammed shut, right in front of her face. Although there was no physical contact between her and the doors (well, maybe a few bristles were pruned off the end of her nose), she stepped back and began teetering like the last skittle when you think you've scored a strike. Then she tried to steady herself by making strange hand gyrations which just make her look silly, as though she were playing invisible maracas, then WUMP! Down she went like a mighty sequoia felled by chainsaw.

The sound of muppet on concrete sent shivers through my very soul. It was not dissimilar to an old carpet being thrown out of a first floor window and was immediately followed by the tinkle of trinkets that sprayed out of her handbag. She just lay there, quite unable to get up, just looking around at her spilled oddments. At least a turtle that's been flipped on to its back doesn't have to concern itself with the whereabouts of its lipstick and vanity mirror.

I was the first on the scene to help her to her feet. The driver of the bus also got out his cab to help. He was a Polish chap from a different depot and couldn't speak a word of English, so it was just as well I was there to lend a hand. After giving the muppet a brief once-over, we were amazed to find no cuts, grazes or broken bones. With double airbags as standard, muppets must surely be the safest mode of personal transport. Think that's a pot-belly? Wrong – it's a front impact crumple zone. Think that's a walking stick? Wrong – it's a titanium anti-roll bar. Yes, Glasgow muppets are quite indestructible. In fact, I'm pretty sure they would even give cockroaches a run for their money following a nuclear war.

We gathered up all her trinkets and helped her on to the bus. All she said throughout the whole ordeal was, 'The driver went too fast! The driver went too fast!' No, actually the driver didn't move an inch, but I doubt that will count for much when she lodges a complaint against him. Or her son lodges a complaint on her behalf when he hears about it. Or a 'concerned onlooker' lodges a complaint just because they haven't lodged a complaint for a while. Or all three.

A few moments later, driver Gurglegulp turned up with my bus. I told him that Chucklemumble had been bagged last week but he seemed unconcerned. It quickly transpired that he was preoccupied with more libidinous pursuits: 'Is Stingball still playing his porn DVD in the bothy?'

'Well, yes. But, I think Chucklemumble is going to appeal his sacking. That was just out of order,' I said.

'Which one is it? Is it the one with the midgets runnun' aboot with masks on and then the chubby woman takes a whole can o' Pepsi?'

'Erm, I think so.'

'Yes! She reminds me of Driver Hippogonk. I'll have tae get a copy o' that!'

Well, so much for driver unity.

I set off into town. Fortunately the passengers were all fairly normal, which came as a relief following my little talc-puff of excitement at the bus stop. I still couldn't believe the muppet had fallen over without even so much as a nudge. It must be that bus auras are highly poisonous to muppets if they can topple them from a distance. Bad feng shui or something. I had come to believe that even the phonetic pronunciation of the word 'bus' had the same destabilising effect on muppets as trombones have on clowns. Complete constitutional failure.

Mercifully, I got normal passengers all the way through the city centre and down Caledonia Road, but my luck eventually ran out in that loathsome lobster pot known as Fernhill. Three neds and a nedette barged on to the bus, each with a bottle of Buckfast in a blue polythene bag and juvenile all day ticket. Strangely, the three neds all wore exactly the same mischievous grinny-frown on their faces, as though the front of their heads had been stamped by the very same paint-dipped potato.

But no painted spud could explain the aloof manner of the nedette. Despite her rampant acne, she was suspiciously expressionless. She gave nothing away and that worried me. I've learned that just because there aren't any ripples in the water doesn't mean there isn't a crocodile watching you just under the surface. There was definitely hidden evil there and all it took was a few sips of Buckie to unleash it.

They supped on their 'broon wine', also known in Glasgow as 'wreck-the-hoose juice', at the back of the top deck like all good neds do. It was still fairly early in the evening and I could sense these neds were struggling to contain themselves despite being outnumbered by normal passengers. But as the journey continued, and the number of normal passengers dwindled, the party began to flow. There was chipmunk music from their mobile phones, crazy stomp-dancing up and down the gangway and all the windows had been opened for a good old smoke.

'Driver, you'll need to get them seen to,' said a normal passenger as he came down the stairs to leave the bus. 'They're smokin' weed an' drinkin' Buckfast and noo they're trying to set fire to seats.'

'Ahh! That'll be him with the flame thrower, then,' I said, looking at my CCTV monitor at the ned with a five inch flame coming out of his lighter. Sure enough, my nostrils were suddenly greeted with a mixture of dope and smouldering bus upholstery, reminding me of when I threw a dead hedgehog on to a bonfire when I was a kid. Pungent yet carpety.

I hit the emergency radio button and was patched straight

through to the radio controller. 'Neds with Buckie and dope, now setting fire to seats! Send the police!' I said and gave my location. He read back my message to confirm everything was correct before signing off to phone the cops. However, the radio volume was extremely loud on this particular bus and the neds upstairs must have heard every word because they became very agitated.

'Here! That fuckin' driver just called the pigs!' shouted one of the runts.

'No he never!' shouted another.

'Aye, he did!'

'Here! Driver! Did you just call the fuckin' pigs?' shouted a ned down the stairs. I ignored him. 'Here! Driver!' I continued my ignoring. 'Driver! Did you call the pigs? You're a rocket by the way!'

Fearing the worst, the neds and nedette began furiously grabbing all their neddy paraphernalia together at the back of the bus. In the confusion, the nedette bumped into a normal passenger in a snorkel jacket who was by this time thoroughly pissed off with the neds and all their neddy nonsense. There must have been an exchange of words because I began hearing shouts and screams and, as I watched my CCTV monitor, fists started to fly. BIFF! Within seconds I was watching a full-scale bar room brawl.

Unfortunately, poor Mr Snorkel was getting the shit kicked out of him. One of the neds even had time to start videoing the assault while his colleagues (including the nedette) punched and kicked their cowering victim. The police would probably take ages to turn up and although I wanted to help, there was no way I was getting out my cab in case a knife was pulled. Things didn't look good for Mr Snorkel.

Then, from out of his seat came a huge hulking brute of a man, the kind of monster who eats raw meat and shits vegetables. I noted an Irish accent when he boarded at Rutherglen and remember thinking, I bet Mr O'Brick wrestles bulls. He clearly sympathized with Mr Snorkel's plight and decided to make free with his fists in the direction of the neds, pummelling them asunder like a locomotive chewing on a car that tried to sneak across a level crossing. Smackety smack! Delightful!

Even better is that neds are consummate cowards. Now with a real fight on their hands, they crapped their tracksuit bottoms and tried to flee, but the punishing fists of O'Brick and the newly resurgent Mr Snorkel just wouldn't hear of it. Although the nedette had already fled down the stairs, the three remaining neds were given the choicest bruises and bashes to remember when they tried to follow. In fact, O'Brick leaned down the stairwell and grabbed the last ned by the scruff of his tracksuit top, dragged him back up and mashed his face with a final salvo of knuckles. Truly the cherry on the cake.

'There's a guy up there assaulting ma pals, driver!' screamed the nedette at me through my bandit screen.

'Don't worry,' I said, 'the police are on their way and you can explain it to them.'

'Ha! Ha!' she barked up the stairs. 'The polis are comin! Ye're for it noo, ya prick!'

'Let's just get tae fuck!' shouted a ned as they barrelled down the stairs and off the bus.

'No! I want tae get the polis to that prick!' insisted the nedette.

'Just run!' called the neds, and that's exactly what they did. They ran. Not down the street, but like true yellow-bellies they bolted straight into nearby bushes.

Right in the chops! I think he'll need a back scrubber to clean his teeth from now on.

I decided to go upstairs and check everyone was okay. As well as Mr Snorkel and Mr O'Brick, there were a few Miss Marples and Murder, She Wrotes babbling away in a state of shocked delirium. They were really quite hysterical. Imagine a nun returning to find a mystery turd in her cloister, knowing the only other person with a key was Mother Superior – that's the kind of trauma we're dealing with here.

'You guys alright?' I asked.

'One of those wee arseholes hit me o'er the heid wi' a boattle!' said Mr Snorkel.

'Do you want the police?'

'No! Get them tae fuck!' he laughed.

O'Brick said nothing.

Fair enough. After inspecting the large holes that the neds had burned into the back seat with their lighter, I went back down into my cab and told Control what happened. Because the freak of neds had left the bus, they decided to cancel the police and just made me continue in service as though nothing had happened. Pah! There should be an optic filled with Smirnoff beside the ticket machine so that drivers can steady their nerves after such lawlessness. From what I've heard, Polish drivers have got it right with their hip flasks and shot glasses. Make mine a doubleski, comrade!

Thanks to the hold up, I was now late and the bus running ten minutes behind had caught up. I had a look to see who was behind the wheel and, as luck would have it, it was the newly demoted Jelly Baby. Brilliant! This was just what I was waiting for. I put on my hazard warning lights and transferred my passengers to his bus.

'There's been a fight on my bus and I need to wait here for the police,' I said and watched his face drop. It was only a little white lie but it was so worth it to give him more work to do. With me off the road, he would have twice the number of punters to pick up and would have a full standing load in no time.

I waited until his bus was out of sight and then just slunk along behind him. It's not nice being shafted, is it Jelly Baby? Yes, I shafted the brute all the way into East Kilbride and all the way back again. Both decks of his bus were absolutely heaving and I could almost hear his punters snapping at him because they had to stand. It was wonderful. Any notion of having consideration for one's fellow driver was shafted out of me long ago by Stingball (and others) and this opportunity to get revenge on Jelly Baby for laughing off my earlier complaint was just too good to miss. Even the anxiety I felt as a new start when Jelly Baby had hit me with route after route I didn't know came back to strengthen my vengeance. 'Life's a bitch,' he had said, 'now go drive!'

Now whose life's a bitch? Get it right up ye, knucklehead!

27
THE GRASS

Despite what you might read in these pages, many bus journeys are incredibly dull. Apart from getting paupers to sing 'Twinkle Twinkle Little Star' and firing lemmings out my emergency door to liven up long, monotonous shifts, I have also invented a bus driving game for my own pleasure – Wobble Head. It's quite simple to play. Just accelerate the bus to about 30mph and jerk the steering wheel a few inches to the left, straighten up, then jerk a few inches to the right. Seeing thirty skulls bobbing to and fro has a delightful slapstick quality which has me howling in the cab every time. It's a bit like watching a tennis crowd at Wimbledon, except I know that it's always me scoring the aces.

Another good use for Wobble Head is keeping drunkards awake when you see them sliding down their seat into a coma. Most drivers hate the high jinks involved in rousing a sleeping oaf at the terminus, so a few sharp Wobble Head jerks along the road can be as good as if you had slipped a ProPlus into their beer yourself.

Tonight, I was Wobble Heading out of my skin in order to keep an inebriated dullard from going under. He was an older geezer who had been a complete bastard since getting on my bus at Gallowgate. After snatching his ticket from the machine, he knocked on my bandit screen and said, 'Hey, driver! Have the decency to wait till I sit doon, will

ye?! That last driver I got just shot away an' made me fall
o'er an' I nearly broke ma fuckin' ankle!'

I just stared at him. This unkempt yo-yo was in his late
fifties and looked as though he had just been spat out of a
tornado. Everything was everywhere – wild hair, wild eyes,
and, if his soiled attire was anything to go by, a wild fancy
for bog-snorkelling. Everything about this scruffy little
rumpler reminded me of the devastation I beheld after my
house was ransacked by burglars. It's not often you meet
someone whose appearance makes you want to cancel your
credit cards and get a rottweiler. But everything really was
everywhere. Alcohol had clearly befriended this guy, gained
his confidence, then flipped him upside down and shaken
him mercilessly by the ankles.

*A lesson for us all: no matter how shit your life, never suckle at the yellow tin
boob. She'll have your legs away every time.*

Despite waiting until he was safely seated before I moved off, Mr Twister immediately shuffled himself back down to my cab for another blast of hot air. 'What is it wi' all youse bus drivers?' he shouted.

'What do you mean?' I asked.

'See that stoap where I got oan back there?'

'Yes.'

'Last week when I got the bus from that stoap, a wee wumin got oan there wi' her wee dug. But the driver comes oot an' says, "Hey! Ye cannie bring that dug on tae the bus withoot a leash!" But the wumin says, "It's only a nice wee doggie an' it'll no bite anyone!" But the driver says, "No! Get yer dug aff the bus!" So the wumin comes doon the bus and spits right in the driver's face! I mean right in his face! The driver says, "Get tae fuck ya' durty bitch!" and the wumin runs aff the bus. Then the driver goes, "Right! That's me been assaulted! I'm goin' aff ma shift! Everybody get aff the bus!" and he paps everybody aff the bus at the side o' the road and drives away! I thought that wuz bang oot of order! Is he allowed to dae that?'

'Well,' I said, 'if I came into your work and spat in your face, what would you do?'

'I don't work, I'm on incapacity! Ha! Ha! Ha!'

Just as I was about to get really sarcastic, I became somewhat distracted by a flash of headlights in my mirror. A ned-mobile had pulled up next to me at the traffic lights, blaring those awful smurftastic chipmunk tunes. All four neds had KFC bags on their knees, but instead of munching on their tasty nuggets, they appeared to be nibbling on the paper bag that contained said nuggets. What were they up to?

'Well, I think it wuz bang oot of order what that driver done!' protested Mr Twister as he tottered away up the bus.

Just as the traffic lights turned green, the neds intentions became clear. The little bastards used their straws as blow-pipes to fire wet blobs of chewed up paper at my cab window. Then, with a snorty laugh and a wheel spin, they were gone.

'The wumin shouldnae huv spat in the driver's face, but for Christ's sake, he shouldnae huv papped us aff the bus!' muttered Mr Twister, still seething. 'He wuz just bein' a bastard! That's all there is tae it!'

Mental note: *Keep cab window closed at ALL traffic lights.*

Next time I checked my CCTV monitor, I found Mr Twister seated but slouching down lower and lower. I tried everything to stop him from losing consciousness, but despite all my best Wobble Head antics, not to mention deliberately striking kerbs and flying through a roundabout at thirty-five miles per hour, the bastard was now snoring into his belly button. Damn it!

I did not relish the prospect of trying to awaken this grouchy old dreg at the terminus. God only knew how he might react. When a filthy grenade lands next to you, your natural instinct is to run away, not poke it. So I resorted to slightly more aggressive tactics; I slammed on the brakes, hit the accelerator then slammed on the brakes again. Despairingly, this just made him slouch further down his seat. I tried again, harder, but I must have been a bit too violent because next time I checked the CCTV monitor, he had disappeared!

If flinging him from his seat could not rouse him then I had to hold my hands up and admit defeat. Rigor mortis had obviously set in faster than I thought. This meant that when I finally arrived at the Baillieston terminus I had to get out my cab, walk up the back to where Mr Twister was lying on the floor and just boot him awake.

'Whu? Humph! Fk! Buh!' he said, along with many other poetical abstractions.

'Wakey! Wakey! You're at the terminus!'

'Huh? Where's that?'

'Caledonia Road.'

'Where's that?'

'Baillieston.'

'DON'T YOU FUCKIN' FANNY ME ABOOT!' he shouted, pulling himself up. Now, Baillieston is hardly Oz, but Mr Twister looked every bit as traumatised as Dorothy waking up to an orgy of munchkins and giant lollipops.

'I'm not fannying anyone about,' I said. 'I'm due back at the depot in fifteen minutes and you'll have to get off here and wait for the next bus.'

'FUCK OFF! I'm no standin' oot there in the dark on ma tod! You can take me back tae Parkheid right noo!'

'I'm not going anywhere near Parkhead. I'm going 'Not In Service' down the motorway. This is the end of the line, you'll have to get off.'

'I'm no goin' anywhere!' he barked, and flumped down in a chair and folded his arms.

'Are you not getting off?'

'NO!'

'Fair enough,' I said and put the bus into gear. I drove him round the Baillieston loop, up to the main road and parked the bus right across from Baillieston police station.

'Oh, so you've brought me here, have ye?' he said with a discernible tremble in his voice.

'Aye! Unless you get off, I'm going to honk my horn and two cops are going to come out and take you away.'

'No! Don't, driver! Don't hit yer horn!' he yelled with increasing panic. 'I cannae be seen wi' them! Driver, I'm a grass!'

'You're a grass?'

'Aye! I'm a grass! I tell 'em things! I cannae be seen talking tae them here! I'll get murdered if I'm seen talkin' tae them!'

So, Mr Twister was a police informant! A backstabbing, eavesdropping Deep Throat who would gladly see his associates banged up for the price of a few bottles of whisky. Well, I'm glad to see the cops are using credible and reliable sources of intelligence to fight crime in our neighbourhoods. We can all sleep better at night for that.

I couldn't resist playing with him a little before I let him go. Never before had I considered my bus horn to be a minister of death, but just to freak him out, I tapped it lightly with my fist, just enough to make it 'meep' a few times. Again, his reaction was all munchkins and lollipops. But, I think if a bus driver held my life in his hands, mine would be too.

The novelty eventually wore off and I just let him go. Finally, I arrived back at the depot for the same drill as always. A wee Oompa Loompa wearing an orange boiler suit came aboard and removed the cash box, then I parked the bus ready for The Tuba to come on with her magic broom. But there was another guy stoating around the yard with a high viz jacket and a clipboard. At first I thought it was Cloth Ears, but as the diesel fumes cleared, I was surprised to see that it was Gollum.

'You alright, then?' I shouted. 'Heard you got clobbered by the East Kilbride Young Team?'

'So they tell me! I don't remember anythin' aboot it. Don't even remember phonin' the ambulance. All I remember was the paramedic askin' me all sorts o' daft questions, like 'What year is it?' and 'Who's the Prime Minister?' They were trying tae find oot how many brain cells I had left.'

'You alright now? I heard from Chucklemumble that you'd wrapped the job.'

'I have,' said Gollum. 'The drivin' at least.'

'So what you doing now if you're not driving?'

'They've got me doin' wee odd jobs aboot the depot yard, checking buses and stuff. They want me to go back tae the drivin' coz they're always short of drivers, but there's just nae way in hell I'd ever go back tae that shite! Besides, you should see some of the young Polish cleaners they've got in here at night. Well tasty!'

I thought it a shame that his driving career had been cut short because of a bunch of mindless thugs. Being reduced to doing odd jobs around the yard must really have been hitting him in the wallet too. However, if I saw any old Volvo Olympians rocking from side to side in the yard in the near future, I'd know why. Nasty Nancy had, thanks to greater European unification, become Nasty Nanski.

28
THE RAWEST NERVE OF ALL

'Ha, ha, ha! I've just shafted Jelly Baby all the way tae Paisley and all the way back into the city!' guffawed Driver Weepingclown as he burst through the door of the bothy. 'I just bent him o'er like this,' and he made the actions, 'I pulled oot ma boaby like this,' and pretended to unzip his flies, 'and just pumped his wee fat arse all the way doon Paisley Road West,' he made as if to hump the table over which he had just thrown Jelly Baby's imaginary rump, 'and all the way back again,' he humped with greater vigour. 'Yeah! Squeal like a piggy! Yee haaaaa!!'

It seemed impossible to escape hardcore pornography when you were in the bothy. Even though female Driver Hippogonk had got Stingball into trouble with The Manager for playing his dodgy skin flicks, here was the Weepingclown acting out a scene from *Deliverance* right in front of our eyes. There were roars of approval from other drivers in the bothy, including myself, who had all been screwed over by Jelly Baby at one time or another. He had used each of us for his sport, now we were using his rear end for ours.

I was coming to the end of my first year as a bus driver and should not have thought when I started that I would be exulting over other drivers' lives being made a misery. Despite having quite egalitarian beliefs when I joined the company, I quickly realised that my colleagues would have not the slightest twinge of conscience about doing so to me either. Despite the friendly banter in the bothy, it really was every man for himself out there.

After finishing my Pot Noodle, I headed out to pick up my bus. Driver Humpty pulled into the stop with only a handful of punters. 'It's absolutely dead out there,' he said, peeling himself out the cab.

'Good, good. By the way, I hear your sparring partner, Ubu, got fired.'

'Aye, good riddance. He was just a big smelly arsehole,' said Humpty. I knew it! He was heartbroken.

However, as I climbed into the cab, I figured Humpty should have been that last person on Earth to complain about big smelly arseholes. When you're in the cab for five hours, and your staple diet consisted of curry and kebab meat, was it too much to ask that you crack the window open before your relief picks up the bus from you? Damn it! But anyway, according to Humpty, it should be a nice quiet run which was always a bonus.

Yes, 'should be'.

'Driver!' came a rasping voice at St Enoch Square. 'Gonnae wait on ma burd? She's just come oot the hospital and she cannae run! Gonnae wait on her, big man? Eh? Hurry up, for Christ's sake!' he shouted over his shoulder.

Every time I drive through the city centre, I always seem to pick up *someone* whom I fear will ultimately become a nuisance to other passengers. They are usually quite easy to spot (and smell). But even on the rare occasions when their appearance and odour are quite inconspicuous, their untamed potty-mouth will always give them away.

'Fuckin' mooooove!' he yelled up the street. I think tonight's *someone* was going to be him.

He was a bumbling little junkie who was weighed down

with several plastic bags containing the day's thievings. Although he considered himself to be quite normal and just like everybody else going about their daily business, his ragged countenance suggested much hidden knavery. Indeed, his mug seemed to have bits missing from it. It was as though he had an attack of the midnight-munchies last night but couldn't be bothered walking to the fridge. So he just lay there and nibbled at his own face. Those terrible corrugations in his chin could really have just been teeth marks in the cheese.

His 'burd' eventually dithered into view. Like her fella, she probably considered herself to be just another normal pedestrian making for the bus. But what the world actually saw was an unkempt ratty calamity, as pale as a geisha but not nearly so willing to please. She bumbled along, banging into lamp posts and street signs as one eye chased the other around her head in a googly methadone waltz. This gaunt hustler was a twiggy artist's easel, draped in threadbare denims with Edvard Munch's *The Scream* cross-eyed upon its shelf.

At last, Face Muncher and The Scream stepped on to the bus. Without so much as a nod or a wink, The Scream floated right past me and took herself up to the back of the top deck. Face Muncher put his bags down and made as if to search his pockets for change. 'Right, where the hell is it? (grope) I've got ma change here somewhere, driver. We're goin' tae Summerston, by the way (grope). See, she's just oot the hospital an' that, know what I mean? I've had tae go up tae the hospital tae get her. There was all that shit goin' on, an' (grope) she's got her ain weans in that other hospital, that's where we're goin' later oan. Whit's it called? I'll have tae get everythin' bloody sorted for that, anyway (grope).

Need tae go up an' see her feether tae. Fuckin' bastard, where's ma change?'

Hmmm. Anyone who can transform the simple purchase of a bus ticket into an expletive-rich soliloquy will always merit special attention on my vehicle. Just as well my CCTV monitor was working so I could keep an eye on him and his shenanigans. But secretly, I knew that he did not have any intention of actually buying a bus ticket. He had other skills that a smack habit had sharpened.

'Just let us put these bags up the stairs the noo, driver, and I'll look for ma change, eh? Aye, that's what I'll dae! Back in a minute!' and with that, he gathered up his thievings and humped them up the stairs. And up the stairs he stayed.

I closed the doors and set off, deciding that if he did not come back down with their full fares within two stops, I would eject them both and have a radio call put out to warn other drivers not to pick them up. Yes, it would give me perverse pleasure to ban them from every bus in the fleet at a single stroke and have them marooned in the city centre and – *Aaaaarg!* – and – *Whooaaarg!* – and . . . what the? Right, who the hell was doing all that screaming?

I'd turned right into Jamaica Street and heard the most terrible whooping and yelling coming from upstairs. A quick scan of the CCTV monitor showed that The Scream was on her feet, and yes, she was screaming. 'I am NOT a tramp!' she protested. 'I am a lady and you will treat me like a lady!' Well! I didn't have any spaghetti for them to re-enact that iconic scene, but both being loathsome wretches, maybe a length of ticket roll would suffice. Not as romantic, but infinitely more chewable.

The Face Muncher merely offered his middle finger and a shrill laugh, which rang throughout the whole bus.

Affronted, The Scream immediately turned about and shambled for the stairwell with, 'You're nothin' but a wee wanker!' But by the time her spindly legs brought her down to the lower deck, the Face Muncher was up, out of his seat and quickly on her tail.

'A lady?' he called. 'Look at ye! Have ye seen yersel'? Yer a fuckin' monster!'

'Nooooo! Get away frae me!' hooted The Scream. 'Driver! Open the door, let me away from that prick!'

Only too willing to oblige, I pulled into the stop at McDonalds and opened the door. The Scream bolted like a whippet from a trap and continued to shout obscenities from further down the street. The Face Muncher, however, remained on the bus, standing on the platform with a can of Tennent's in hand, bellowing ferocious obscenities while crowds of people stopped and stared.

'Pooh!' he hollered, wafting his hand under his nose as if consumed by a sudden stench. 'Yer fanny's mingin'! (waft) (waft) Yer fanny's mingin'!'

'Oh my God! You're gettin' stabbed! I'm gonna get Jamesie tae stab yoo! You're gettin' rubbed oot!' screeched The Scream.

'Ye've got crabs an' yer fanny's mingin'! Pooh! (waft) I can smell ye frae here!' shouted the Face Muncher even louder, just in case anyone on Jamaica Street missed it.

'You're deid!' she replied.

Eventually, The Scream scuttled out of sight and the Face Muncher took himself and his beverage back upstairs. He seemed quite pleased with himself as he sipped at the dregs and made small talk with whoever would listen. Very strange behaviour for a man who'd just been mortally cursed. But I believe his smugness stemmed from the knowledge that

According to the Face Muncher, it wasn't just the lips on her face that were screaming.

only an insult that cut to the rawest nerve has the power to illicit a death threat. And, based on their exchanges across Jamaica Street tonight, I'd say he had penetrated to the rawest, most unsanitary nerve she had. Bullseye!

A few minutes later . . .

(Knock, knock.) 'Driver!' came a shout from a short, scraggy muppet at my bandit screen.

'Yes?'

'There's a man lying on the floor, upstairs. I think he's unconscious. I just thought I'd let you know.' Then she shuffled away back up the bus and sat down.

I had a pretty good idea who she was referring to. Not too sure how to handle a snoozing junkie situation, I drove on for a bit hoping that some idea would present itself, but nothing came. Perhaps it would be best just to wait until I got to the Summerston terminus and the bus was empty before going upstairs to rouse the punk. But my hand was forced by that scraggy little muppet who came back down the bus and knocked on my bandit screen once again.

(Knock, knock.) 'Driver, did you hear me?' she husked. 'There's an unconscious man lying on the floor upstairs. You'll need to do something! There're people up there, for goodness sake!'

She had evidently become quite enraged by my inaction and stood there glowering at me. Although only four feet tall, she looked to me like the complaining type, the most dangerous species of muppet by far. Her complexion accorded perfectly with her demeanour – dry and withered yet spongy, as though a sudden shower of rain would have her swelling up to twice her normal size. An erect muppet would probably shoot twice the number of complaints too.

I observed, with creeping nausea, the deep crevasses around her lips. Many long years of cigarette sucking had creased and folded the lower part of her face into an arid rectal pout. It was quite ruined.

Although I rebuffed much of her goody-two-shoes bullying, other passengers were now complaining to me about this 'stinking man lying in a heap on the top deck'. With great reluctance, I yielded to their pleas and agreed to go upstairs and investigate. Risking a loaded hypo in the face was actually preferable to suffering the scorn of a whole army of muppets. I would take it easy, though – no Gollumesque heroics.

With trepidation, I climbed the stairs and was almost overcome by the heavy funk of stale beer and urine. The expression on the faces of the few passengers who had managed to stay upstairs and bear it was that of serious retch-fatigue. I strode quickly past them and came upon the figure of Face Muncher lying on his back. On one side. his bag of thievings, and on the other, a can of Tennent's which had been knocked over and lay in a puddle. A bit like Face Muncher himself. In fact, I couldn't help but notice that with his arms and legs spread out like da Vinci's *Vitruvian Man*, it was as though he had succumbed to sleep whilst making snow angels in his own piss.

'Wakey, wakey!' I shouted down at him. But no response. 'WAKEY, WAKEY!' (BOOT) But still he did not stir. He just lay there with his mouth agape, doing the best impression he could of a filthy French squat-over-a-hole-in-the-ground type latrine. After a lot more shouting and even more booting, without any success whatsoever, I decided that this menace was going to require more manpower to shift.

'I'm afraid I'm going to have to get him seen to,' I said to the upstairs passengers. 'I'll need to get the cops to him.' With that, they all stood up and walked dejectedly and somewhat grumpily down the stairs and off the bus.

'What's going on up there, driver?' asked Mrs Ciggy-Sucker, with eyes that were more ravenous for gossip than Fuzz Claw's. She was waiting for me as soon as I walked back down the stairs towards my cab. I announced that I was going to wait here for assistance in removing Sleeping Beauty from my floor. Her little face just dropped as all the passengers on the lower deck sighed, stood up and stormed off to get another bus. That's right, you should have kept your wee puckered mouth shut and let me deal with this at the terminus, then everyone would still be going. Silly muppet spoiled it for everyone. She probably got lynched at the bus stop for that.

But getting the cops wasn't so easy. My bus radio was broken for starters and I didn't have my mobile phone with me. When I flagged down another bus and asked the driver to call for assistance on my behalf, it quickly became apparent that the Pole couldn't understand a single word I said. Damn it! If I couldn't get the cops to come to me, then I'd go to them. So I put up 'Not In Service' and drove the vehicle off-route and round to Partick police station.

After explaining the situation to a nice blond she-cop behind the desk, two large oafs were summoned to do my bidding. As the three of us walked out to the bus, I noticed that the rest of Partick police station was hanging out of upstairs windows to see what was going to happen. I didn't realise a junkie ejection could pull such a crowd.

As soon as the cops boarded the bus, they let loose with 'Oh, my God! I can smell him from here!' They walked up stairs and booted the Face Muncher's feet and shins around a bit. When this didn't work they pulled at his ear lobe. Just at the point where I was sure his ear was going to rip off completely in the cop's hand, he barked and opened his eyes.

'Aargh! Get tae fuck!'

'C'mon, wake up, pal!' shouted the cops.

'Talkin' aboot? I've got a ticket . . . somewhere!'

'You're not welcome on the bus, you'll need to get up,' said a cop.

'Wait a minute, where the hell am I?'

'You're outside Partick police office.'

'Partick? You're frickin' kiddin' me! I'm goin' tae Summerston! Whit have ye brought me here for?'

Both cops must have had enough at this point because they grabbed the Face Muncher and hauled him to his feet. All the time, he clutched his bags of thievings close to his chest. As he was huckled downstairs, I overheard him demand a free lift to Summerston, or at least a taxi fare for all the inconvenience he was being put to. 'Besides,' he said, 'ma missus is just oot the hospital and I need tae get hame and see tae her!'

I was rather hoping the police would wink at me as a secret signal that they were going to take him away into the police station and rough him up a bit just for being a wretched turd. Unfortunately, they didn't. Once off the bus, they just talked to the guy calmly at the side of the road as though they were long time acquaintances. Damn it! They were just going to let him go! Now *that* was perhaps the rawest nerve of all.

After the Face Muncher had calmed down a bit, he confessed the real reason why he was in such a hurry to get to Summerston: the rest of his booze was hidden in a hedge and he was fearful that all that 'fuckin' Young Mob' would find it. The police advised him that he had already drunk too much and they were concerned for his wellbeing. But the Face Muncher was resolute, 'No! This is nothin' for me. I'm usually far worse than this! See this one time, Ah wus mair drunk than Ah've ever been in my puff. Ah remember walkin' up the stairs tae ma flat wi' ma mate and Ah fell o'er and heard this almighty crack. Ah didnae know whit it wuz but I saw all this blood. When ah felt ma face, ma nose wuz still there, but ma teeth wurnie! Ha! Ha! Ha! Ma mate telt me Ah wuz pure squeelin'!'

Ouch!

I took my reeking bus back to the depot and expected at least a wince from The Tuba when she came aboard with her bucket and magic broom.

Nothing.

No display of emotion whatsoever – she didn't even furrow

her brow as she set about the stomach churning mess. The Tuba would make a formidable poker player. Much better than Driver Ticklemop, who just happened to be passing and stepped onto my bus to say hello. His entire face just curled in on itself like a frightened hedgehog and he let out a prolonged 'Jeeeeeesus!' I told him my story about the filthy junkies and he listened avidly. 'That's one for the bothy!' he said. But knowing Ticklemop, he'd probably try to pass it off as one of his own.

29
FACE SLAMMER

Driver Hippogonk was almost in tears in the bothy. She was still a new driver and was finding it difficult being thrown in at the deep end. 'I didnae know the bus route last night,' she said, 'so I asked the punters, but they just took me the wrong way doon a wee alley for a laugh and I couldnae get back oot! Then they started fightin' wi' other people on the bus coz they were complainin' aboot it. I don't think I can dae this any mair! I go hame every night crying tae ma man and he says, "I'm goannie go in tae that depot the morra an' stab somebody!" but I told him "No! It'll get better", but it's no getting any better at all!'

Poor Hippogonk. Although I could sympathize completely, there were no words of comfort that could be offered. That's just the way things were when you were new. Unfortunately, going out into the dark on the late shift never really got easier with time.

With me having been in the job for a whole year now and seen violence and vandalism up close, I had learned to expect it but could never get used to it. I would pray for howling wind and lashing rain to keep people off the streets when out driving late so they stayed at home and didn't cause me any trouble. Scotland was supposed to have really lousy weather – not lousy enough if you ask me.

Mind you, it had been a wonderfully quiet night so far. With a forbidding chill in the air, there was mercifully little yob-loitering for bus drivers to endure. Good thing too, because my route took me away from the main arteries and through the shadowy nooks and crannies of the city's most desolate ghettos. Trying to inch a full size bus through those cramped and twisting streets can often leave you open to petty meddling and even all-out ambush by the local tribeschildren. This was truly a ramble through Glasgow's dank basement.

Tonight's steed was an old Volvo single decker, a real battle-scarred veteran. Every dimple and impact crater in its bodywork was evidence of numerous previous sorties. Just as I returned to the cab after moving aside some traffic cones that had been strategically positioned in the middle of the road by the Young Parkhead Rebels – who were now fortunately nowhere in sight – the bus radio crackled into life.

Incoming Radio Message: *Central control to all services in the vicinity of Stobhill Hospital. Be on the lookout for a male, approximately twelve years old, short black hair, slim build. He's absconded from the hospital and he might try to get on a bus. If he gets on your bus contact control immediately. He's quite easy to spot because he's got an intravenous drip in his arm. Control out.*

You have got to be kidding! I've heard hospital food ain't that good, but Jesus! On second thoughts, he was probably just a silly ned who thought it would be a good idea to climb out a window and fill the drip-bag with his favourite tipple – good ol' Buckfast. Sure, sticking it in an intravenous drip gets you liquored up a lot faster, but an empty drip-bag is not nearly as useful in a fight as an empty bottle of Buckie.

Threatening to strike your foe over the head with an empty plastic bag simply does not carry the same menace.

My route did not take me a million miles away from Stobhill and I secretly hoped that drip-boy would cross my path so I could find out why he was so desperate to escape the manky clutches of our National Health Service. A clue offered itself at the very next stop. No, it wasn't drip-boy, but a horrific, raggy, gap-toothed crone whose legs were rendered quite useless by ale. She was flanked by a younger woman and a man who were frantically flagging down my bus while trying to support her limp little body.

With great reluctance, I stopped and opened the doors. Without any fare being offered or even so much as a nod, the young couple frog-marched the crone on to my vehicle and dumped her on the seat behind my cab. 'Make sure she gets aff at the Loudern Tavern, driver!' said the man, and then he left the bus. The crone made some groaning, burbling noises.

So, she was my burden now, was she? Well, thank you very much! Did the sign on the front of my bus say, 'Bring Out Your Dead'? Mind you, she was so wasted that I probably wouldn't have her for long. It was just a question of when she would fall off her seat and crack her skull open. Then she'd be just another melty-faced mong who'd drunk herself into the back of an ambulance. If it really was hideous peasants such as she who were devouring our healthcare system, then no wonder drip-boy bolted from Stobhill. It was simply the shock of finding himself surrounded by such savage murderers of their own health. An overnight stay in a Glasgow hospital can be more viscerally shocking than a six-monther in Barlinnie. As Stingball would tell you.

So be it. I started off down the road, driving as carefully as possible so as not to throw her from her seat. But a little voice in her head must have commanded that she go down and show the driver her bus pass. So, she slithered off her seat, landed on the floor and slowly crawled on all fours down the bus to my cab. Eventually, some tufts of hair and a pair of googly eyes emerged beside my cab door. 'Dat's my pass, driver,' she slobbered, and held up her transcard.

'Thank you,' I said, and pulled into the side of the road so she could more easily crawl back up the bus and pull herself back into her seat. My only other passengers were a teenage girl and a middle-aged bloke. Both seemed highly amused with the crone's display and watched avidly to see what she would do next. They did not have to wait long.

I pulled away from the kerb, accelerating as gently as I could, but at the very first bend in the road:

BANG!

'Oh, my God!' shouted the young girl. I looked round to see the drunken crone had slid off her seat and slammed her head into the bus floor. She just lay there, in a crumpled heap, with eyes half-shut, gurgling. I stopped as both the man and the girl leapt up and lifted the crone back into her seat. Very community spirited of them but I couldn't help feeling that it was a mistake. Of course they wanted to help, but they should have left her where she was for her own safety. After all, if you saw someone bashing their own brains in, you wouldn't place the bat back in their hands if they dropped it.

'Are ye alright, noo?' asked the man, once he had perched her back onto the seat.

'Aye, I'm alright,' groaned the crone.

'Are ye sure? Yer no goannie fall aff yer seat again, are ye?'

'No,' said the crone.

We set off once again into the night. After a couple of

minutes, the man pressed the bell to signal that he wanted off. As I slowed down and pulled in to the bus stop:

BANG!

The crone had taken another nosedive into the floor. I caught that one in my passenger mirror and observed that she made absolutely no attempt to break her fall or stop her head from taking the full brunt of the impact. Her mobile phone and other trinkets spilled out of her handbag, but she seemed completely oblivious to this and just lay there in a heap, like a puppet whose strings had been cut. The man once again lifted the rag-doll back into her seat. This guy was a sadist.

'Thought ye said ye wurnie goannie fall again?' he said, gathering up her trinkets and placing them back in her bag. 'Are ye sure ye're alright?'

Gurgle-burble, went the crone, unable to even hold up her head.

'Good luck with than one, mate! Ha! Ha!' he said to me as he left the bus. 'Fuck havin' your job!' he added.

Funny, that's just what I was thinking. After he left, I closed the doors but did not release the handbrake. I knew that just as soon as the bus started to move, the drunken wretch would probably take another dive. So, what to do? I couldn't sit here all night and wait until she sobered up. Maybe tie her to a seat somehow? Or maybe just leave her at the side of the road and inform the cleansing department? Just as my thoughts started to get really inhumane:

BANG!

I hadn't moved the bus an inch, but down she went again, this time bursting her nose open and leaving a pool of blood on the floor. My one remaining passenger, the teenage girl, jumped up and made as if she were going to pull the blood-bearded hag to her feet, but she recoiled upon seeing the red liquid.

'Are ye alright, doon there? Have ye hurt yer nose?' she asked.

The crone looked up and struggled to focus. 'Are . . . you . . . the . . . polis?' she mumbled.

'No, I'm only nineteen!' said the girl.

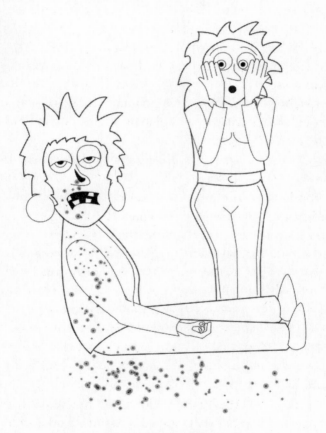

Are you the polis?

Unexpectedly, the crone made a valiant effort to pull herself up, seemingly unaware that her gushing nose was spilling down her denim jacket. Over the course of a several minutes, using handrails, and a little support from the girl, she just managed to wobble to her feet. I wasn't sure if that was such a good idea. Placing any distance at all between her head and the floor was just asking for more trouble.

'Make sure she gets her arse into a seat quickly,' I shouted. But it was too late.

BANG!

Ooh! That was the loudest yet. This time she ripped open the bridge of her nose and made bubbles with the blood that ran into her mouth. The young girl stepped over her, 'Driver, goannie just let me oot?' she asked, now quite flustered.

'Are . . . you . . . the . . . polis?' burbled the crone once more, face down in her own coagulating goo.

'No, I'm not the polis! I'm only nineteen!' said the girl. 'Driver, please just goannie let me oot?'

'Aye, fair enough,' I said and opened the doors. Can't say I blamed her. The girl left swiftly and now I was alone with the crone. I put up 'Not In Service' on the destination screen so that no one would try to get on, then called Central Control and requested an ambulance. All I had to do now was babysit the blood-soaked wraith until the paramedics arrived.

I just sat in my cab behind the safety of the bandit screen in case she moved suddenly and sprayed me with her juice. But she just writhed around on the floor, moaning. After a while, some tufts of hair gradually appeared beside my cab door, followed shortly by two lifeless eyes. The rest of the face that appeared was very different to the one that rose up previously to show me her transcard. It was bruised, bloodied and utterly abased.

'Take me tae the Loudern Tavern!' groaned the face.

'No way, the bus is staying here,' I said. 'Besides, I think you've had enough to drink tonight already.'

'Whit? Fuckin' let me oot, then!'

'No, you're staying here until the ambulance arrives. You're not getting on any other buses tonight.'

'Open the fuckin' door!'

'No! If I let you out, you'll just end up getting knocked down in the road.'

'Whit's it tae you? Eh? Ya bastard! Whit's it tae you?'

Not a great deal to be perfectly honest. If she wanted to get completely blitzed, smack her head around and then get run over by a truck, then c'est la vie. But now that she had embroiled me in her night of debauchery, I felt the need to wind things up with as little form filling as possible. I was actually shocked at how my sense of sympathy and compassion for the city's pathetic souls had numbed over the course of this year. For sympathy and compassion were exactly what many of them preyed upon, and I had none left. Give them an inch and they'll take a mile. My journey to the dark side was now complete.

While this thought jarred in my mind, the ambulance pulled in and a paramedic emerged. As he busily put on a pair of latex gloves, I hoped the crone would at least behave herself for him. I opened up and he stepped aboard. Stooping down to the ruined figure on the floor he said, 'What's your name, sweetheart?'

Mumble mumble, went the crone.

Mr Paramedic shone a torch in her face. 'Aye, you've got a wee cut on your nose. C'mon in to the back of the ambulance and we'll get you seen to.' He patiently helped her up. Whatever they're paying these guys it's nowhere near enough.

'She'll be alright then, will she?' I called after him as they shuffled towards the ambulance.

He turned. 'Oh, aye! She's just guttered!' he said. I sensed from his tone that paramedics suffer their own emotional numbness too.

A thought occurred to me as I drove the blood-spattered bus back to the depot. If the drip-boy who earlier absconded from Stobhill finally decided to sneak back in through his hospital window (now with the inevitable alcohol poisoning from his Buckie filled drip), he'd probably find that a drunken crone with a bandaged up nose had been given his bed. There would just be something wonderfully poetic about that.

I drove into the yard and parked the bus. The Tuba stepped aboard and paused when she saw the blood all over the floor. She looked at me and, without a word, she grimaced. She actually grimaced! For a split second there was a look of utter disgust on her face. But then it was gone, her natural composure returned and she set about the bus floor with an old rag. It had taken a whole year, but I had finally managed to bring a bus back to the depot that even The Tuba found downright repugnant. I would treasure that grimace in my mind forever.

Gollum was walking around the yard with his clipboard and spied my bloody floor. 'Blood? You'll need tae fill in a report aboot that in the depot. I'll need to mark it doon tae,' and he scribbled on a piece of paper.

Did I hear him correctly? Fill in a report? This was the same Gollum who had previously told me not to fill in any paperwork after an incident because I would just be incriminating myself. The very same Gollum who had warned me what Management did to honest drivers. I could see what was happening here. Ever since he gave up driving and took up his clipboard after being clunked over the head by the East Kilbride Young Team, Gollum had softened. In the safety of the depot, he had forgotten what it was like out there. Dealing with managers every day, Gollum had become a Company man. For me, that was the saddest twist in his demise.

'Thcrew the report! Theh! Theh!' called a voice that was all chuckle and all mumble.

'What the . . . ? You're back?' I said, and hopped out the bus.

'Aye! Juth thtarted back today,' said Chucklemumble as we walked to the depot office to sign off. 'Back by popular demand. Theh! Theh!'

Well, that was something. Maybe the Union wasn't a complete waste of time after all. Now in the depot office, there were several other drivers milling around. The one with the beard and spectacles turned round, his stare lingered upon us. Before Chucklemumble and I had a chance to catch up, the driver interposed with, 'Thought you got sacked?'

'I did,' said Chucklemumble, 'but I appealed through the Union and won, and noo I'm back.'

'Did they let you keep your service?' asked Kisses.

'No. Back to zero. They put me back doon on tae the thtarter rate of pay too. Bathtardth! Twenty yearth ethperienth and I'm on rookie money!'

'So that means you're officially a new start then, doesn't it? You're a virgin! You know what I do to new starts, don't you?'

'Oh, no! Don't you thtart that! Get away frae me!'

Driver Kisses cornered Chucklemumble right there in the depot office and planted a big furry smacker right on his cheek. 'If I knew that wath gonna happen I would have thtayed thacked! Theh! Theh!' said Chucklemumble. I very quickly signed off and left. Although I now had a year's service under my belt, compared to most other drivers in the depot I was still a foetus. And I sensed Driver Kisses was feeling frisky tonight.

30

TERMINUS

Laphroaig is a strong single malt whisky that has a bouquet of creosote and goes down like tar. You will balk upon taking your first sip as the pungent kick of the peaty aroma assaults your unprepared senses. However, swirl it around your mouth for a while and you'll experience the sweet nuttiness of the barley and a distinct heathery perfume. It takes a whole bottle to get used to, but you'll discover the bottle will empty quicker than you think, as you go back to it again and again.

Over the past year, I discovered that bus driving was very much like a bottle of Laphroaig. It felt like a kick in the balls to begin with when you're simply given a bus and told to, 'Go drive!' But after you master the routes and develop a thick skin to the violence and vandalism, it was just possible to also have a little bit of fun out there too. Despite occasionally going home with a very bitter aftertaste, I just got used to getting up the next day and pouring myself another shift. And another. And another.

I'm not sure how long it will be before the inevitable hangover kicks in, but considering there are many drivers in the depot who have been doing the job longer that I've been alive, I think it's going to be a very long party.